GLP-1 MEALS made easy

75+ Recipes and Nutrition Advice for Your Weight Loss Journey

Aliza Olive, MD, and Kellie Bader, PharmD

Callisto Publishing LLC

Published by Callisto Publishing LLC C/O Sourcebooks LLC
P.O. Box 4410, Naperville, Illinois 60567-4410
(630) 961-3900
callistopublishing.com

Recipes originally published as *The Mediterranean Diet* (2013), *The Complete Ketogenic Diet for Beginners* (2016), *Diabetes Cookbook and Meal Plan for the Newly Diagnosed* (2018), *Eat What You Love Diabetes Cookbook* (2018), *The High-Protein Bariatric Cookbook* (2020), and *The High-Protein Vegan Cookbook for Athletes* (2021) in the United States of America by Callisto, an imprint of Callisto Publishing LLC.

Text by Andrew Leigh
Photographs by Evi Abeler
Author photos courtesy of Hilary Fuller Images

Art Director: Lisa Schreiber
Art Producer: Stacey Stambaugh
Editor: Mo Mozuch
Production Editor: Rachel Taenzler
Production Designer: Jeffrey Piekarz

Cataloging-in-Publication Data is on file with the Library of Congress.

Printed and bound in the United States of America.
VP 10 9 8 7 6 5 4 3 2 1

GLP-1 MEALS MADE EASY

For you, the person who is done with diets that fail you. You're choosing GLP-1s plus smart nutrition. You're enhancing your weight loss, health, and life. We're cheering you on!

CONTENTS

INTRODUCTION

We are Dr. Aliza Olive, a pediatric critical care physician and ethics researcher, and Kellie Bader, a pharmacist and certified nutrition coach. Together, we co-founded GLP1 Enhanced to help people using GLP-1 medications such as Ozempic, Wegovy, and Zepbound lose fat, preserve muscle, and build lifelong habits that support a healthy metabolism.

If you are holding this book, you have already taken a meaningful step forward. Maybe you are unsure what to eat now that you are rarely hungry. Maybe your weight is coming off, but you feel tired, weak, or frustrated about how your body looks. Or maybe you are realizing you need to take control of your actions instead of leaving it up to the medication alone. Whatever brought you here, we are so glad you came.

GLP-1 medications are powerful, but they do not come with a road map. That is why we created this book: a clear, practical guide to help you nourish your body, support your goals, and feel your best during every stage of your journey.

Inside, you will find a guide to help you build your own 21-day meal plan and a collection of simple, high-protein, healthy-yet-tasty recipes designed specifically for GLP-1 users. These meals are built to work with your shifting hunger cues, support digestion, and help you feel strong and satisfied.

We have coached thousands of people on GLP-1 medications to optimize their results with proper nutrition, and we have walked through it ourselves. After struggling with fatigue, bloating, and that "skinny fat" feeling, we both rebuilt our strength, metabolism, and body composition by changing how we approach food. No extremes. Just the right foundation.

We want that for you, too. Let this book be your next step. You do not have to be perfect. You just need a plan. And now you have one!

HOW TO USE THIS BOOK

This book is designed to support you from the inside out. In part 1, we give you an overview of how GLP-1 medications work and how to use nutrition to optimize fat loss. You will also find a flexible guide to help you build your own 21-day meal plan, one that supports feeling full, energized, and on track without overthinking it. Part 2 is packed with simple, delicious recipes that are high in protein, blood-sugar friendly, and designed to work for individuals managing diabetes or weight loss.

Use this book as your go-to resource. Start where you are now and build from there. No need to make a 360-degree change in your diet that you won't be able to keep up with after two weeks. You've got this!

Part One

GETTING STARTED AND MEAL PLANNING

We know how overwhelming it can be to start a new medication, especially one that changes how you feel about food. That is why we designed the first part of this book to help you feel grounded, informed, and ready to take action.

In chapter 1, we walk you through what to expect with GLP-1 medications. We will explain how they work and what side effects are normal. You'll learn how to use food to protect your metabolism, preserve muscle, and support long-term fat loss.

In chapter 2, we talk about more than food and discuss how sleep, exercise, and hydration all impact how you feel. This chapter is about giving you a deeper insight into what's going on inside your body so you can understand where you'll see changes and how to plan accordingly.

In chapter 3, we get straight into the good stuff with a simple, doable framework to help you build your own 21-day meal plan. This is not a strict diet. It is a flexible foundation built around high-protein meals that will keep you full, fueled, and feeling amazing.

We have helped thousands of people use this exact approach to hit their weight-loss goals. Now it is your turn, and it is going to be easier than you think.

CHAPTER 1

The Skinny on GLP-1s

This chapter is all about laying the foundation. If you are using a GLP-1 medication, you have likely noticed some big shifts already. You may feel full faster. Your cravings may have quieted down, or maybe the food noise you thought was gone is starting to creep back in. And perhaps you have lost weight but are not quite loving how your body looks or feels. Sound familiar?

GLP-1 medications work by changing how your body handles hunger, blood sugar, and digestion, and even how your brain responds to food. These changes can be powerful tools, but they work best when you know how to use them. That is where we come in. We will explain how these medications work and what you can expect physically and emotionally. More important, we will show you how to support your body with food that helps you feel stronger, not weaker. Leaner, not just smaller. Energized, not exhausted. Satisfied, not depleted.

We know food has been a source of stress for many of our clients, especially during or after they reach their weight-loss goals. Our goal with this book is to help you turn food into a powerful tool, not a source of confusion or guilt.

By the end of this chapter, you will have a clear understanding of what is happening inside your body, why certain foods matter more now, and how to start building habits that support your goals for the long haul. This is not just about losing weight. It is also about gaining confidence, peace of mind, and a better relationship with food. And this time, you can do it for good.

UNDERSTANDING GLP-1S

This section gives you the foundation you need to understand your medication and use it effectively to support your goals. You'll learn the basics behind these medications as well as common side effects and benefits. Odds are your doctor has gone over these basics with you, but even if that's the case, this section can be a valuable refresher.

What Are GLP-1s?

Ozempic, Wegovy, and similar prescriptions are all part of a class of medications known as *GLP-1 receptor agonists*. These were originally developed to help people with type 2 diabetes manage blood sugar. GLP-1 stands for *glucagon-like peptide-1*, a hormone that helps regulate insulin. In addition, the peptide slows digestion and signals fullness to the brain. When researchers saw how well the secondary effects of these medications reduced appetite and reduced food noise to create a calorie deficit resulting in weight loss, it became clear that GLP-1s have broader benefits beyond diabetes management.

A common myth is that GLP-1 medications are brand new and that we know little about their long-term effects. In reality, the first GLP-1 was approved in 2005. Ozempic (semaglutide) was approved by the U.S. Food and Drug Administration in 2017 for the treatment of type 2 diabetes. Wegovy, its higher-dose counterpart, was later approved specifically for weight loss in people with obesity or weight-related medical conditions. Similar medications, such as Mounjaro and Zepbound (tirzepatide), soon followed.

Although these drugs started in the diabetes world, their impact on hunger, cravings, and food consumption has made them popular tools for weight loss. Now, more people than ever are using GLP-1s to improve their health and take back control of their bodies.

How It Works

GLP-1s work by mimicking the GLP-1 hormone, which plays a key role in blood-sugar control, appetite regulation, and digestion. When you eat, GLP-1 helps your body release insulin, which lowers your blood sugar. It also slows down how quickly food leaves your stomach, so you feel fuller longer.

That slowed digestion is one reason people on GLP-1s often find themselves eating less without trying. You feel full faster, and that feeling lasts. On top of that, GLP-1s act on the brain to reduce cravings and quiet constant thoughts about food, something many people describe as "food noise."

All these effects work together to support fat loss: better blood-sugar control, fewer cravings, and a stronger signal from your body when it has had enough. You are not just eating less. You also are making more mindful choices about food, which is exactly what makes this tool so powerful.

Common Benefits

GLP-1s are best known for helping people lose weight, but the benefits actually go far beyond the number on the scale. One of the biggest medical advantages is improved blood-sugar control. By increasing insulin production and slowing the release of sugar from the liver, these medications stabilize blood glucose levels, especially after meals. This is beneficial for people with type 2 diabetes or those at risk of developing it.

Another important benefit is cardiovascular protection. Clinical studies have shown that GLP-1s can reduce the risk of major heart-related events, such as heart attacks and strokes, in people with type 2 diabetes and heart disease. For many users, weight loss is just one part of a bigger health transformation.

Together, these benefits, such as fat loss, better blood-sugar regulation, and improved heart health, make GLP-1 medications a great option for people looking to manage their weight and improve their long-term health.

Side Effects

As with any medication, GLP-1s come with side effects. The most common are gastrointestinal, such as nausea, bloating, constipation, diarrhea, and a general sense of food "just sitting there." Some people also report fatigue, dizziness, or changes in taste. These symptoms are especially common during the first few weeks. This is why it is so important to start with a low dose and go up slowly. You may also notice an increase in side effects after a dosage increase.

The good news is that most of these side effects tend to subside over time as your body adjusts. Eating smaller portions, staying hydrated, choosing easily digestible foods, and moving your body, especially by walking, can make a big difference in how you feel.

While most side effects are manageable, it's important to know what to watch for. Some users experience changes in mood, including anxiety or depression, while others may develop gallstones if weight loss occurs too quickly. Diarrhea, though less common than constipation, can also occur. This list is not exhaustive, and if you feel off or worried, it is always a good idea to check in with your provider.

Before we dive into specific food strategies, remember: This book is here to help you feel better. The recipes and meal plan are built around gentle, high-protein, fiber-rich foods that aid digestion and match your new appetite. You are not alone, and you do not have to figure it out by trial and error.

Can I Take GLP-1s Forever?

This is one of the most common questions we hear, and the answer is not one-size-fits-all. GLP-1s were originally designed for chronic use, particularly for people with type 2 diabetes. That means, yes, they can be taken long-term. In fact, studies such as the Semaglutide Treatment Effect in People with Obesity (STEP) program have shown that people tend to regain weight when the medication is stopped, especially if they do not have a clear plan for sustainable change.

But here is the thing: Just because you *can* stay on a medication forever does not mean you have to. We have worked with thousands of individuals who successfully tapered off GLP-1 medications or reduced to a maintenance dose without regaining the weight. What made the difference? Building healthy habits, promoting muscle growth, increasing metabolism, and finding your new maintenance energy before stopping the medication. Long-term success depends less on how long you take the medication and more on what you do while you are on it. GLP-1s give you a window of opportunity with less hunger, fewer cravings, and more mental space to practice a new way of eating. But if you stop without a plan, your body's old patterns will return.

Whether you choose to stay on your GLP-1 for years or just a season, our professional advice is the same: Use this time wisely. Nourish your body, protect your muscles, and lay a solid foundation. That will give you the freedom to decide what is next for you, and, most importantly on your terms.

SETTING REALISTIC GOALS

We will explore how your relationship with food impacts your mindset, energy, and long-term success. Our goal for this section is to help you feel strong, confident, and in control of your progress every step of the way.

Weight Loss

Most people see noticeable changes in the first three months on GLP-1s, often losing a few pounds per week, especially early on. By six months, many have lost 10 to 15 percent of their starting weight. At one year, studies show an average weight loss between 15 and 20 percent. But the scale numbers do not tell the whole story.

Non-scale victories matter just as much as the number on the scale. Improved energy, looser clothes, reduced cravings, improved labs, and less joint pain are all signs your body is thriving. Focus on how you feel, not just what you weigh. This is where real, lasting change happens, and that is what this book is here to support.

Energy and Wellness

While some people feel more energized as the pounds come off, others may feel tired or sluggish at first, especially if they are not eating enough or are adjusting to smaller portions. While GLP-1s may improve sleep and reduce inflammation over time, slower digestion can also cause bloating or discomfort early on.

The key is to stay hydrated and nourish your body with high-protein, nutrient-dense meals. Gentle movement, such as walking, can ease digestion and boost energy naturally. If you feel off, it does not necessarily mean something is wrong. It may just mean your body is adjusting. Give it time and take care of yourself.

Medical Goals

Regular follow-ups with your healthcare provider are essential while taking GLP-1s. Your doctor will likely monitor key labs such as A1C (to track blood-sugar control), kidney function (since some medications are cleared through the kidneys), cholesterol, and electrolytes. These values help ensure the medication is working safely and effectively for you.

As weight comes off and inflammation decreases, you may see improvements in blood pressure, cholesterol, and insulin sensitivity. These are major wins that do not show up on the scale. Stay connected with your care team. They are there to help you adjust your plan and celebrate every health milestone.

Psychological

Over the first few months on medication, you likely will notice a shift in how you think about food. GLP-1s reduce hunger and food noise, so many people feel more in control and less emotionally driven to eat. This is your chance to break old habits by creating a new rhythm for yourself.

Diets often rely on willpower and short-term rules and restrictions. A true lifestyle change happens when you learn to fuel your body, not punish it. Food is not just fuel, but also part of holidays, celebrations, and culture. Practice embracing the enjoyment that food can bring along with the balance of honoring your body. As you create your new path, you should start to see food as something that helps you reach your goals, not something to battle against. That is real freedom.

GLP-1 MYTHS DEBUNKED

This section clears up some of the most common myths about GLP-1 medications. From fears about muscle loss to expectations of a magic fix, we will separate fact from fiction so you can move forward with confidence and clarity.

You Stay on Them Forever

While GLP-1s are approved for long-term use, that does not mean you must take them forever. Some individuals with chronic conditions such as type 2 diabetes may benefit from continued use. Others choose to use GLP-1s as a temporary tool to lose fat, build habits, and reset their metabolism.

We have helped many clients taper off medication without regaining the weight, but only after they have built a strong foundation through nutrition, strength training, and habit change. With the right plan, it is absolutely possible to preserve your progress without staying on medication for life.

They're Only for Diabetics

Although GLP-1s such as Ozempic were originally developed to treat type 2 diabetes, they are now FDA-approved, under the brand name Wegovy, for weight management in individuals without diabetes. These medications support weight loss through mechanisms that improve both insulin sensitivity and appetite regulation.

Because obesity and diabetes are closely connected, treating one often helps improve the other. GLP-1s help interrupt the cycle of overeating, insulin resistance, and inflammation. Whether you are managing blood sugar or trying to prevent future health problems, these medications offer powerful benefits for many people, not just those with diabetes.

They're "Cheating"

This is one of the most persistent misconceptions we hear, and one we love to bust. Taking a GLP-1 is not cheating. It is a strategic choice to use an available tool that can help you succeed. Yes, GLP-1s can make weight loss easier by reducing hunger and cravings so you can keep yourself in a calorie deficit. But that does not mean the process is effortless. You still need to fuel your body wisely, prioritize protein, stay active, get enough sleep, and manage stress with consistency.

We have seen many people lose weight on GLP-1s without building good habits, only to regain the weight when they stop the medication. The truth is that success requires effort, consistency, and a mindset shift. Using a tool to promote your health isn't cheating; it's smart, strategic, and absolutely something to be proud of.

CHAPTER 2

Your Body on GLP-1s

If you have started a GLP-1 medication, you probably already noticed that things feel different. Perhaps your appetite disappeared overnight. Perhaps your digestion slowed down. You may be eating less but feeling more tired, slightly dizzy, or not quite like yourself. These changes are real, and they are a direct result of how GLP-1s work in your body.

This chapter is here to help you understand why those shifts happen and what you can do to feel your best while your body adjusts. From changes in hunger and fullness cues to shifts in energy, sleep, and even mood, we will walk you through what is normal, what needs attention, and what you can do today to feel stronger and more in control.

The good news? You have more power than you think. Small choices, such as eating enough protein, drinking more water, walking daily, or getting more sleep, can significantly impact how you feel while using this medication. Fueling your metabolism, protecting your muscle, and feeding your body well will not only help you feel better each day, but will also prepare you for long-term success, whether you stay on the medication or plan to taper off.

This chapter provides a deeper look at how GLP-1s affect digestion, hydration, and body composition, along with strategies we have used with thousands of clients to help them thrive. We are not just talking about surviving the side effects. We also are focused on helping you optimize how you feel and function. You deserve to feel good in your body while you work toward your goals. Let us help you make that happen.

YOUR BODY ON GLP-1S

This section explores how GLP-1s change the way your body feels, sometimes in unexpected ways. From reduced appetite to shifts in digestion and energy, we will break down what is normal, what to watch for, and how to aid your body as it adjusts.

Metabolism

GLP-1 medications transform your appetite by mimicking your body's natural fullness hormone. This slows digestion, keeping food in your stomach longer, which then signals your brain that you are satisfied, even after a smaller portion. While many people experience a noticeable decrease in hunger, it is still essential to nourish your body with high-protein, nutrient-dense meals.

Prioritizing protein supports satiety, preserves lean muscle mass, and protects your metabolism. By leveraging your medication's appetite-suppressing effects in a thoughtful way, you can promote sustainable fat loss and lay the foundation for maintaining your results, even if you taper down or go off the medication.

Not everyone experiences complete appetite loss. Some still feel hunger or notice it returning quickly between meals. If that's you, don't worry; it's normal. Focus on high-volume, high-fiber meals with protein and vegetables to keep you full longer. Eating satisfying, balanced meals can help reduce the urge to snack without ever feeling truly satisfied.

Dehydration

A reduced appetite often leads to lower fluid intake. When you eat less frequently, you may forget to drink altogether. Fullness can also make drinking uncomfortable, increasing your risk of dehydration and electrolyte imbalance. You may even mistake thirst cues for hunger.

You may need more water than you think. Many clients aim for 10 to 12 cups a day. Lightly salting meals or adding an electrolyte-enhanced beverage can help maintain hydration. If plain water feels difficult to tolerate, try lightly flavored options with lemon, cucumber, or mint. Staying hydrated improves metabolism, digestion, and energy levels, helping you feel your best throughout your GLP-1 journey and beyond.

Gut Health

A slower digestive process is one of the most common side effects of GLP-1 medications. Many people experience bloating, constipation, or the sensation that food is simply not moving through their system. These symptoms are common early on and usually subside with a few simple changes.

Aid your gut by eating fiber-rich foods such as berries, leafy greens, beans, and whole grains. Drink water throughout the day and make time for gentle movement, such as short walks after meals. If symptoms are severe or persistent, consult your healthcare provider. With the right approach, most digestive discomfort can be managed effectively.

Overcoming Nausea

Nausea is a frequent side effect of GLP-1 medications, especially during the first few weeks or after a dosage increase. The slower digestion caused by the medication helps you feel full longer, but it can also lead to bloating or queasiness.

Additional triggers include sugar alcohols, which are often found in sugar-free snacks or protein bars; these can worsen bloating, gas, or diarrhea for some people. A sudden increase in dairy, such as yogurt or shakes, may also contribute to discomfort, especially if you're lactose-sensitive. Skipping meals entirely can sometimes backfire, leaving your stomach empty and more prone to nausea.

You can also reduce nausea by eating smaller, slower meals. Avoid greasy, spicy, or heavy foods, particularly earlier in the day. Instead, try bland, easy-to-digest options such as toast, crackers, broth, rice, or applesauce.

Sip fluids slowly rather than all at once. Ginger tea, ginger chews, or ginger capsules are natural remedies that often help.

Many of our clients find it helpful to eat a small protein-based snack, such as a few bites of Greek yogurt or a hard-boiled egg, just before taking their medication.

The good news? Nausea usually diminishes as your body adjusts. Be patient, listen to your body, and remember: You can always talk to your provider if symptoms become severe or persistent. You do not have to push through discomfort alone.

HOW GLP-1S MAKE YOU FEEL

By now, you have likely started noticing changes in appetite, digestion, and thirst. We will walk you through practical tips to stay nourished, hydrated, and comfortable so you can feel strong, energized, and in control while your body adjusts to your GLP-1 medication.

Appetite

If food has become an afterthought, it helps to shift from eating only when hungry to eating with consistency. On GLP-1s, skipping meals may feel natural, but doing so can lead to fatigue, dizziness, and muscle loss over time. Set a reminder to eat every four to five hours, aiming for three meals per day, even if they are small. Build each meal around protein to help preserve muscle and support satiety. Keep quick, easy options on hand, such as hard-boiled eggs, yogurt, or protein shakes. Eating consistently will reinforce the habits you will rely on later, when hunger returns.

Thirst

When your appetite drops, your thirst often does, too. GLP-1s slow digestion, which can dull thirst cues and lead to dehydration and mild electrolyte imbalances. You may not feel thirsty, but you still need water, and likely more than you think. Stay ahead of dehydration by sipping water regularly throughout the day, not just at meals. Keep a water bottle nearby as a visual reminder, and take small sips often. Don't wait until you feel thirsty, because you might not.

Add a pinch of sea salt to your food or include a low-sugar electrolyte drink to improve hydration and electrolyte stability. If you feel dizzy, constipated, or low in energy, check your fluid intake. Staying hydrated is one of the simplest and most effective ways to improve how you feel on GLP-1s.

Digestion

Digestive changes are common side effects of GLP-1 medications. Slower gastric emptying can cause bloating, constipation, or a sensation that food is not moving through your system effectively. While uncomfortable, this is a normal part of how the medication works.

For better digestion, eat smaller meals, chew thoroughly, and avoid greasy or overly rich foods. Incorporate fiber-rich options such as berries, lentils, and leafy greens, and drink plenty of water. Walking after meals can also reduce discomfort and promote regularity. If symptoms persist or become severe, speak with your healthcare provider. Relief is often possible with a few strategic adjustments.

DEFINING WELLNESS

Losing weight is only one part of the puzzle. True wellness runs deeper. It is about feeling energized, confident, calm, focused, and emotionally resilient. The most successful transformations combine nutrition, movement, rest, and stress relief. When medication and food choices are paired with a full wellness routine, both body and mind can thrive.

Why Exercise Matters

You do not need to live in the gym to benefit from movement while using GLP-1s. Even light activity helps with digestion, protects muscle, improves mood, and helps with fat loss. Movement does not need to be intense to make an impact.

If you are not currently active, begin with something easy. Take a short walk each day. Do a few stretches in the morning. Try a ten-minute online video or a brief bodyweight routine. The goal is not perfection; it is consistency. As your strength and energy build, so can your efforts. Movement is one of your best tools, and it is never too late to start.

Building a Wellness Routine

Wellness is not about just food and exercise. It is about how you care for your entire self. Chronic stress increases inflammation, disrupts sleep, and often leads to emotional eating. Small habits such as deep breathing, journaling, or stepping outside for a few minutes can help reset your nervous system and quiet your mind.

Begin the day with one small win. Something as simple as making your bed or drinking a glass of water can set a positive tone that can snowball your entire day. When you start to rely on momentum that *you* create on your own with a simple morning win, you will no longer need motivation, which is fleeting. Wind down in the evening with a few minutes of calm. These little moments build emotional resilience and can reshape how you feel, mentally and physically.

Get Some Sleep

Sleep is a powerful ally for fat loss and overall health. When you are not sleeping well, your hunger hormones increase, your cravings intensify, and your metabolism slows. Some people on GLP-1s notice changes in sleep patterns, such as vivid dreams or light sleep, especially early in treatment.

Good sleep hygiene makes a difference. Stick to consistent sleep and wake times. Avoid caffeine late in the day. Dim the lights and unplug from screens at least an hour before bed.

Try reading, stretching, or listening to calm music instead. If rest still feels hard, focus on one small change at a time. A well-rested body recovers better, digests more efficiently, and provides steady energy, digestion, and mood throughout the day.

How to Move with Limited Mobility

If walking or standing for long periods is difficult for you, you are not alone, and you are not without options. Movement looks different for everyone. The goal is progress, not perfection. Find ways to move that feel safe and sustainable.

Chair-based exercises are a great starting point. Chair yoga can improve flexibility and circulation while calming your mind. Seated resistance work using bands or light hand weights can build strength in the arms, shoulders, and core.

Small movements, such as seated leg lifts, arm reaches, or ankle circles, keep your blood flowing and joints active. Even five minutes of exercise can improve your energy and confidence over time. Focus on what you can do, not what you cannot. And if you are unsure what is safe, check with your healthcare provider. Remember, progress is not all or nothing. You deserve to feel strong right where you are.

YOUR NEW NUTRITION

GLP-1s change your appetite, but smart nutrition powers your body. This section will help you learn how to fuel yourself intentionally so you preserve muscle, stay energized, and genuinely enjoy what you eat. It is not about eating less. It is about eating in a way that fuels your metabolism and overall health during this new phase.

What to Eat

When hunger is low, every bite matters. Focus on meals high in protein, full of fiber, and rich in nutrients. Aim for 30 grams of protein per meal using foods such as grilled chicken, lentils, eggs, or Greek yogurt. Add fiber with vegetables, berries, and whole grains such as oats or quinoa.

Recipes in this book, such as the Sunrise Frittata with Fresh Herbs or Tomato Tuna Melts, are simple, satisfying, and designed to meet your body's nutritional needs. Since you are eating less overall, make sure what you eat fuels your energy, aids digestion, and contributes to lasting progress.

What to Avoid

Certain foods can be harder to tolerate while taking GLP-1s. Processed snacks, sugary treats, and greasy meals may contribute to energy crashes, trigger cravings, or make digestive symptoms such as nausea and bloating more noticeable.

Refined carbohydrates, such as chips, pastries, and white bread, are low in nutritional value and can spike blood-sugar levels without providing lasting fullness or benefits. Fried foods and alcohol may also be more difficult to digest, especially while your system is adjusting to slower gastric emptying. You do not need to eliminate everything, but these foods should be enjoyed occasionally, not daily.

Be especially mindful about alcohol. Because food stays in your stomach longer while on GLP-1s, alcohol may absorb more slowly and hit harder. Combined with dehydration and fewer meals, alcohol's effects may feel more intense than expected. Sip slowly, eat beforehand, and check in with how your body reacts.

Focus on the good stuff. Whole, minimally processed foods are rich in nutrients such as vitamins, minerals, and fiber. They tend to be more filling, maintain steady blood sugar, and help you get more nutritional value from every bite, which is especially important when you are eating less overall.

What to Know About Food Now

Focus on eating full meals rather than grazing all day. Snacking can keep you from ever feeling satisfied, while a complete meal with protein, fiber, and healthy fat can help regulate appetite and reduce cravings.

There is plenty of room for flexibility and enjoyment, but quality matters. A day of sugary snacks might fit your calorie quota, but it will not give you the nutrients, stamina, or blood-sugar stability you need. Choose options that taste good and help you feel strong, focused, and well.

CHAPTER 3

The 21-Day Meal Plan

Welcome to your 21-day meal plan, designed to help you lose fat, maintain muscle, and feel amazing while on your GLP-1 medication. No matter what your goal, this plan is your starting line.

We're beginning with a complete, done-for-you Week 1 menu. Every meal and snack has been tested and adjusted to hit a rough target of 1,350 to 1,550 calories and 100 to 130 grams of protein per day. (Don't worry; if your calorie goal is more than this, we've got you covered.) You don't have to count macros or wonder if your meals are working; this plan already does that for you. Each day's menu is built to keep you nourished, full, and on track, with enough variety to keep things interesting and flexible.

Why protein? GLP-1s keep you feeling full longer, so you eat less. That makes every bite more important. Protein is the key to preserving muscle mass, keeping your metabolism high, and making your weight loss sustainable, not only while you're losing weight on the medication, but also long after. Each day of this plan contains enough protein to hit that goal. Fiber-rich vegetables, whole grains, and healthy fats round out each plate for balanced blood sugar and long-lasting energy.

The shopping list and prep instructions make execution easy. You'll find overlap in ingredients so you can buy in bulk (things such as chicken breasts, Greek yogurt, and egg whites). The prep list will walk you through how to get ahead before day 1 even begins, such as portioning out smoothie ingredients into freezer bags. The more you prep up front, the easier it will be to stick with the plan through the week.

After week 1, we'll show you how to build your own week 2 and week 3 plans using our recipes. You can mix and match breakfasts, lunches, dinners, and snacks using our plug-and-play formula, which helps you stay on target no matter your taste preferences or schedule. With the right foundation, and a little flexibility, you'll learn how to eat for life, not just for the next few weeks. Let's get into it.

Note: This is not a personalized nutrition plan. It is not intended to diagnose, treat, or prevent any condition, and it should not be used as a substitute for individualized advice from a licensed dietitian or medical provider. Always consult with your healthcare team before making significant changes to your eating habits, especially if you have a medical condition, food allergies, or specific dietary needs.

WELCOME TO YOUR MEAL PLAN

Welcome to Week 1! This is just an idea to get you started. We did not include any meals out, but we did try to incorporate leftovers. How many leftover servings you have will of course depend on the size of your family and how many people are eating each meal. We tried to simplify the list as much as possible to accommodate how groceries are sold. For example, we know you can't buy individual servings of fresh herbs, so whatever package size is available will do. For some produce, we included the option of pre-prepped ingredients as a time-saver. You can double up a recipe and rely on leftovers for more of the meals to streamline your week even more.

	BREAKFAST	LUNCH	DINNER	SNACK	ADDITIONAL SNACK
MON	Sunrise Frittata with Fresh Herbs **Page 36**	Chicken Tortilla Soup **Page 53**	Skillet Chicken with Asparagus and Quinoa **Page 88**	Lemon-Coconut Protein Balls, 2 Balls **Page 155**	
TUES	Sunrise Frittata with Fresh Herbs (leftovers) **Page 36**	Chicken Tortilla Soup (leftovers) **Page 53**	Cashew and Parmesan Crusted Salmon **Page 81**	Lemon-Coconut Protein Balls, 2 Balls (leftovers) **Page 155**	
WED	Egg and Spinach Breakfast Burrito with Fresh Tomato Salsa **Page 37**	Cashew and Parmesan Crusted Salmon (leftovers) **Page 81**	Black Bean Enchilada Skillet Casserole **Page 116**	Peanut Butter and Banana Power Smoothie **Page 148**	Lemon-Coconut Protein Balls, 1 ball (leftovers) **Page 155**
THURS	Egg and Spinach Breakfast Burrito with Fresh Tomato Salsa (leftovers) **Page 37**	Black Bean Enchilada Skillet Casserole (leftovers) **Page 116**	Old-Fashioned Turkey Meatloaf and Mediterranean Oven-Roasted Potatoes and Vegetables **Pages 93 and 135**	Greek Yogurt and Marinated Pineapple **Page 157**	Peanut Butter and Banana Power Smoothie (leftovers) **Page 148**
FRI	Brussels Sprout Hash and Eggs **Page 45**	Thai-Style Chicken Roll-Ups **Page 103**	Spaghetti Squash Lasagna Bowls **Page 101**	Simply Vanilla Frozen Greek Yogurt + ½ cup strawberries **Page 154**	Lemon-Coconut Protein Balls, 1 ball (leftovers) **Page 155**
SAT	Brussels Sprout Hash and Eggs (leftovers) **Page 45**	Thai-Style Chicken Roll-Ups (leftovers) **Page 103**	Quick Weeknight Chicken Parmesan + 2 oz. dry pasta per serving **Page 108**	Cherry Berry Breakfast Smoothie **Page 47**	
SUN	Crispy Breakfast Pita with Egg and Canadian Bacon **Page 46**	Quick Weeknight Chicken Parmesan (leftovers) + 2 oz. dry pasta **Page 108**	Creamy Broccoli and Chicken Casserole **Page 91**	Lemon Meringue Pie Smoothie **Page 149**	

WEEK 1 SHOPPING LIST

Spices and pantry

- ☐ Extra virgin olive oil
- ☐ Balsamic vinegar
- ☐ Rice wine vinegar
- ☐ Nonstick cooking spray
- ☐ Coconut oil
- ☐ Vanilla extract
- ☐ Thyme
- ☐ Oregano
- ☐ Black pepper
- ☐ Ground cumin
- ☐ Salt
- ☐ Turmeric
- ☐ Italian seasoning
- ☐ Onion powder
- ☐ Cayenne pepper
- ☐ Chili powder
- ☐ Rosemary
- ☐ Ground cinnamon
- ☐ Garlic powder
- ☐ Reduced-sodium chicken broth (at least 2 quarts)
- ☐ Whey protein powder
- ☐ Maple syrup
- ☐ Honey
- ☐ 15-ounce can reduced-sodium black beans
- ☐ 15-ounce can cannellini beans
- ☐ 15-ounce can diced tomatoes
- ☐ 16-ounce package tofu
- ☐ 10-ounce can reduced-sodium enchilada sauce
- ☐ Worcestershire sauce
- ☐ No-sugar-added pineapple juice
- ☐ Tart cherry juice
- ☐ 14-ounce jar marinara sauce

Produce

- ☐ 1½ pounds asparagus spears
- ☐ 1 bunch scallions
- ☐ Basil
- ☐ 1 pound spinach
- ☐ 2 pounds cherry tomatoes
- ☐ 5 onions
- ☐ 1 bulb garlic
- ☐ 3 jalapeños
- ☐ 1 Roma tomato
- ☐ 1 medium tomato
- ☐ Dates (at least 3)
- ☐ 3 limes
- ☐ 6 lemons
- ☐ 1 bunch cilantro
- ☐ 1 bunch parsley
- ☐ 1 avocado
- ☐ 2 red peppers
- ☐ 1 green pepper
- ☐ 2 zucchinis
- ☐ 1 banana
- ☐ 8 ounces fingerling potatoes
- ☐ 8 ounces mini red peppers
- ☐ 8 ounces mushrooms
- ☐ 1 cauliflower or 12 ounces cauliflower florets
- ☐ 1 pineapple
- ☐ Mint
- ☐ 1 pound Brussels sprouts
- ☐ Small package bean sprouts
- ☐ 1 head green cabbage or small package shredded green cabbage
- ☐ 1 carrot
- ☐ 2 spaghetti squash (small)
- ☐ 1 pound strawberries
- ☐ 2 ounces microgreens

Nuts/Seeds

- ☐ Cashews (at least 1 cup)
- ☐ Powdered peanut butter
- ☐ Peanut butter (16-ounce jar)
- ☐ Desiccated coconut (at least ½ cup)
- ☐ Walnuts (at least 2 tablespoons)

Grains

- ☐ Quinoa
- ☐ Rolled oats
- ☐ 6-inch corn tortillas (at least 4)
- ☐ Low-carb whole wheat tortillas (at least 8)
- ☐ Whole grain pita bread (one package)
- ☐ Whole wheat breadcrumbs
- ☐ Almond flour
- ☐ Whole wheat flour
- ☐ 1 pound uncooked pasta

Meat/Poultry/Seafood

- ☐ 24 eggs (6 for egg whites)
- ☐ 32-ounce carton egg whites
- ☐ 3½ pounds chicken breast
- ☐ 3½ cups cooked chicken (rotisserie or canned)
- ☐ 8 ounces lean ground beef
- ☐ 1½ pounds lean ground turkey
- ☐ 4 (4- to 6-ounce) salmon fillets
- ☐ 4 ounces Canadian bacon or breakfast ham

Dairy

- ☐ 1 half-gallon unsweetened almond milk
- ☐ Small package feta cheese
- ☐ 4 ounces fresh mozzarella
- ☐ Small package shredded mozzarella
- ☐ Small package shredded Cheddar cheese
- ☐ Small package grated parmesan
- ☐ Small container reduced-fat ricotta
- ☐ 3 (32-ounce) containers nonfat plain Greek yogurt
- ☐ 4 ounces plain goat cheese

Frozen

- ☐ 1 bag frozen pitted cherries
- ☐ 1 bag frozen blueberries or raspberries
- ☐ 1 pound bag frozen broccoli

Prep Instructions

Spend a few hours on the weekend to set yourself up for success. Here's what to do:

1. Chop vegetables such as Brussels sprouts, bell peppers, zucchini, onions, garlic, and asparagus. Store them in containers for easy use.
2. Make the salsa for your breakfast burritos. It keeps for up to three days.
3. Cook and shred chicken to use in the soup, casserole, and roll-ups.
4. Cook 1 cup quinoa (makes about 3 cups) for the Skillet Chicken with Asparagus and Quinoa and the Creamy Broccoli and Chicken Casserole.
5. Roast your Mediterranean vegetables to reheat as sides.
6. Bake the frittata and refrigerate slices for easy breakfasts.
7. Roll the Lemon-Coconut Protein Balls and store them in the fridge.
8. Pack freezer smoothie bags with the fruit, greens, and juice for the lemon meringue, cherry berry, and peanut butter smoothies.
9. Mix the frozen yogurt base and freeze.
10. Optional: Prep the marinated pineapple for yogurt bowls.

That's it! You'll breeze through your meals all week with less cooking and more energy.

WEEK 1 MENU

BREAKFAST:

- Sunrise Frittata with Fresh Herbs (page 36)
- Egg and Spinach Breakfast Burrito with Fresh Tomato Salsa (page 37)
- Brussels Sprout Hash and Eggs (page 45)
- Crispy Breakfast Pita with Egg and Canadian Bacon (page 46)
- Cherry Berry Breakfast Smoothie (page 47)

SALAD AND SOUP:

- Chicken Tortilla Soup (page 53)

POULTRY AND MEAT:

- Skillet Chicken with Asparagus and Quinoa (page 88)
- Thai-Style Chicken Roll-Ups (page 103)
- Quick Weeknight Chicken Parmesan (page 108)

- Creamy Broccoli and Chicken Casserole (page 91)
- Spaghetti Squash Lasagna Bowls (page 101)
- Old-Fashioned Turkey Meatloaf with Sweet Tomato Sauce (page 93)

SWEETS:

- Simply Vanilla Frozen Greek Yogurt (page 154)
- Lemon-Coconut Protein Balls (page 155)
- Greek Yogurt and Marinated Pineapple (page 157)
- Lemon Meringue Pie Smoothie (page 149)
- Peanut Butter and Banana Power Smoothie (page 148)

FISH AND SEAFOOD:

- Cashew and Parmesan Crusted Salmon, served with rice (page 81)

VEGGIE MAINS:

- Black Bean Enchilada Skillet Casserole (page 116)

SIDES:

- Mediterranean Oven-Roasted Potatoes and Vegetables with Herbs (page 135)

Need More Calories?

If you find the sample meal plan isn't quite enough for your needs, it's easy to add on. Try pairing your meals with a calorie- and protein-boosting side, or snacking on things such as hummus and veggies, string cheese, or a hard-boiled egg (or two!). You could include additional recipes from the book as snacks or dessert. Here are some ideas:

- Tropical Coconut Yogurt Chia Bowls (page 49)
- Banana Cream Pie Parfaits (page 144)
- Creamy Pumpkin Pie Smoothie (page 150)
- Chia Chocolate Pudding (page 153)
- Berry Smoothie Pops (page 147)
- Banana Brûlée Yogurt Parfait (page 151)
- Peanut Butter Cup Smoothie (page 156)

These options help you increase your food intake without sacrificing nutrition or satisfaction.

CREATE YOUR OWN WEEKS 2 AND 3

Now that you've experienced a full week of protein-packed, balanced meals, it's time to make this process your own. Instead of asking you to follow a rigid meal plan, we are giving you the tools to build your own based on your preferences, your lifestyle, and your schedule. Whether you want to stick with recipes from this book or mix in your go-to favorites, you'll be able to hit your goals while creating a rhythm that actually works for you.

This approach isn't just more flexible, it's also more sustainable. Most people don't eat twenty-one unique breakfasts or dinners across three weeks. They find a handful of meals they love that fit their needs and that are delicious and easy to repeat. That's exactly what we want for you.

Start with Structure: How Many Meals Do You Need?

Before planning anything, take a look at your week. How many breakfasts, lunches, dinners, and snacks do you realistically need to plan for? Do you work from home some days and prefer to cook in the moment? Do you have leftovers from Week 1 you want to use up? Jot your notes here and use the blank meal planning templates on the following pages to sketch out your week. Once you know what you need, fill in your meals and build your grocery list.

Use the "Repeat and Rotate" Method

To keep things simple and avoid decision fatigue, we recommend bulk prepping one or two breakfasts and one or two lunches that you can rotate all week. This has two big benefits: You save time and energy during your busiest hours, and you make your protein goals easier to hit without reinventing the wheel. Here are some examples:

BREAKFASTS:

Make a frittata, hash, or breakfast bake on Sunday, portion it out, and reheat it all week.

Batch prep smoothies by freezing ingredients in baggies and blending fresh each day.

Mix and match: Alternate between two favorites, such as Brussels Sprout Hash (page 45) and a Cherry Berry Breakfast Smoothie (page 47).

LUNCHES:

Chicken Tortilla Soup (page 53) and Southern Chicken Salad (page 65) store well and can be portioned into grab-and-go containers.

Pasta salads (using protein pasta), hearty veggie bowls, and chili are perfect for reheating or eating cold.

You can double your dinner and eat leftovers for lunch the next day, one of the easiest and most overlooked time-savers. Choose meals you enjoy and don't be afraid to repeat them. If you're not tired of it by Friday, you chose well.

Plan Dinners Around Your Lifestyle

Dinners can be more flexible and creative depending on your schedule. If you have time in the evening, cook something fresh from one of the book's many protein-rich options, such as Cashew and Parmesan Crusted Salmon (page 81), Skillet Chicken and Quinoa (page 88), or Black Bean Enchilada Skillet Casserole (page 116). If you're pressed for time, choose a meal that's quick and easy, or use leftovers from earlier in the week. It's helpful to give your dinners a theme so you don't feel overwhelmed with choices. Some ideas are:

Meatless Monday: Try a high-protein, plant-based main such as the Sweet Potato, Tofu, Chickpea, and Kale Bowl with Creamy Tahini Sauce (page 115) or Falafel with Creamy Garlic-Yogurt Sauce (page 112).

Taco Tuesday: Use chicken, fish, or beans in corn tortillas with slaw and salsa.

Sheet Pan Wednesday: Roast your protein and veggies on a single tray, which leads to minimal cleanup.

Slow Cooker Thursday: Pull out the slow cooker and let dinner cook itself (Apple-Cinnamon Slow Cooker Pork Loin on page 97 is a great option).

Free-for-All Friday: Use up your leftovers or order out mindfully using the "Ordering Out" tips at the end of this chapter.

This book helps you balance your macros without tracking everything. We built Week 1 around the goal of 1,350 to 1,550 calories and 100 to 130 grams of protein per day. You don't need to track every gram of food to keep that rhythm going. As you create your own weeks, keep the following in mind:

Protein is the priority. Every meal should contain 25 to 35 grams of protein, and snacks should add another 10 to 20 grams.

Use the book's recipes. They have been adjusted to hit those protein targets.

Add veggies and fiber-rich carbs. These help regulate hunger, digestion, and blood sugar.

Be mindful of fat and sugar. You don't have to avoid them, but don't let excess cheese, dressings, or sauces crowd out your protein and fiber.

Watch your portions. Especially if you're eating out or using your own favorites, you may need to reduce restaurant-size servings or add extra protein.

Build Your Grocery List

Once your plan is filled out, use the blank grocery list provided to jot down what you need. Group items by section (produce, meat, pantry, dairy, etc.) Don't forget to check your fridge or freezer first; you already may have many staples such as beans, eggs, or yogurt. Want to save even more time? Try this:

- Pick three proteins for the week (such as chicken, shrimp, and tofu)
- Pick two veggies that go with everything (such as broccoli and zucchini)
- Pick two carb/fiber sources (such as quinoa and chickpea pasta)
- Pick one or two snacks (protein balls, smoothies, or Greek yogurt and fruit)

That's it! You've got the base of your week.

YOU'RE IN CHARGE NOW

This is where the plan becomes a lifestyle. Use the blank templates here weekly, monthly, or anytime you feel off track. Having a plan (even a loose one) is one of the most effective ways to avoid decision fatigue, reduce food waste, and stay consistent. You've got the tools. Now it's your turn to play with them.

	BREAKFAST	LUNCH	DINNER	SNACK	ADDITIONAL SNACK
MON					
TUES					
WED					
THURS					
FRI					
SAT					
SUN					

	BREAKFAST	LUNCH	DINNER	SNACK	ADDITIONAL SNACK
MON					
TUES					
WED					
THURS					
FRI					
SAT					
SUN					

Ordering Out

Let's be honest: You're not going to eat at home 100 percent of the time. And you don't need to. Eating out is part of life, and with a little awareness, you can enjoy restaurant meals without derailing your progress on GLP-1 medications.

Start by scanning the menu for protein. Grilled chicken, steak, shrimp, salmon, and tofu are all great choices. Build your meal around one of these lean proteins and then add fiber-rich sides such as a salad, roasted vegetables, or beans. Don't be afraid to ask for swaps; most places will let you trade fries for a side salad or double veggies in place of a starchy side.

Portion control matters more than perfection. Restaurant meals are often double (or triple) what your body actually needs, especially when your appetite is reduced on a GLP-1. One trick is to ask for a to-go box up front and put half your meal away before you even start eating. Another option: Split an entrée with a friend or order an appetizer portion with an extra side of protein.

Appetizers and soups can be your secret weapon. A cup of broth-based soup or a protein-heavy appetizer such as shrimp cocktail or chicken skewers can give you a balanced, satisfying meal without the need for a full entrée.

When it comes to alcohol, moderation is key. GLP-1 medications can make you feel the effects of alcohol more quickly, and drinking on an empty stomach may increase nausea. If you do choose to drink, opt for something simple (such as a glass of wine or a spirit with soda water), and avoid sugary cocktails.

Finally, remember that eating out isn't cheating. You are learning how to navigate real life in a way that supports your goals. Apply the same mindset as you do at home: Focus on protein first, add fiber, and listen to your hunger cues. You're not just following a plan, you're also building a lifestyle. And you can always indulge a little and get right back on track with your next meal.

Part Two

THE RECIPES

We're excited for you to dive into the recipes. The 75-plus recipes you will find in this section were carefully developed to meet every need and preference, with an emphasis on protein and balanced nutrition for your GLP-1 journey. Rest assured, you do not have to be an expert chef to enjoy these recipes. They were created with the everyday home cook in mind.

You likely will find new favorites and go back to them time and time again because they are very doable and can fit seamlessly into your lifestyle. We've also made sure to include foods and meals that you have likely enjoyed for years, just with a healthier spin on them. Look forward to seeing familiar dishes you can continue to enjoy.

CHAPTER 4

Breakfast

Sunrise Frittata with Fresh Herbs

SERVINGS: 3 / PREP TIME: 10 MINUTES / COOK TIME: 20 MINUTES

This frittata is everything we love in a GLP-1-friendly breakfast: packed with protein, full of fresh flavor, and easy to prep ahead. Whether you're sharing it with family on a slow Sunday or meal-prepping it for the week ahead, this dish brings color, comfort, and a metabolism-boosting start to your morning.

- 1 tablespoon extra virgin olive oil
- 10 asparagus spears, trimmed and cut into 1-inch pieces
- 2 scallions, chopped
- 6 large eggs
- 6 egg whites
- ½ cup water
- 2 tablespoons unsweetened almond milk
- 8 large fresh basil leaves, chopped
- 2 teaspoons chopped fresh thyme
- 2 teaspoons chopped fresh oregano
- ½ teaspoon freshly ground black pepper
- Pinch salt (optional)
- 1 cup cherry tomatoes, halved
- 4 ounces fresh mozzarella, cut into bite-size pieces, or 12 small mozzarella balls

1. Preheat the oven to 350°F.
2. In a large oven-safe skillet (preferably cast iron), heat the olive oil over medium heat.
3. Add the asparagus and scallions, and cook for 1 to 2 minutes. Remove from the heat.
4. In a mixing bowl, beat the eggs and egg whites with the water and almond milk. Stir in the basil, thyme, oregano, pepper, and salt (if using).
5. Add the cooked asparagus and scallions to the egg mixture and mix well.
6. Pour the mixture into the skillet. Scatter the tomatoes and mozzarella evenly over the top. Bake until cooked through, 15 to 18 minutes. Cut into slices and serve.

Preparation tip: If you don't have a large skillet, you can sauté the veggies separately and combine them with the egg mixture in a baking dish.

Per Serving: Calories: 336; Protein: 28g; Total carbs: 9g; Fiber: 2g; Fat: 22g

Egg and Spinach Breakfast Burrito with Fresh Tomato Salsa

SERVINGS: 4 / PREP TIME: 20 MINUTES / COOK TIME: 10 MINUTES

A high-protein breakfast that feels like comfort food? Yes, please. This burrito sneaks in leafy greens and keeps you full for hours, which is exactly what you want when you're fueling fat loss or preventing weight regain. Bonus: The fresh tomato salsa adds brightness and flavor without extra calories. Make it ahead to keep mornings simple and satisfying.

FOR THE SALSA

1 pound cherry or grape tomatoes, chopped
½ cup chopped scallions (green and white parts)
2 small jalapeños, seeded and minced
1 garlic clove, minced
⅛ teaspoon salt
Juice of 2 small limes

FOR THE BURRITOS

4 large eggs
2 cups egg whites
⅛ teaspoon salt
¼ teaspoon freshly ground black pepper
1 teaspoon extra virgin olive oil
5 ounces baby spinach
4 large whole wheat tortillas
¼ cup shredded sharp Cheddar cheese
1 avocado, pitted, peeled, and sliced (optional, not included in nutrition information)

TO MAKE THE SALSA

In a small bowl, toss together the tomatoes, scallions, jalapeños, garlic, salt, and lime juice. Cover and refrigerate until ready to serve.

TO MAKE THE BURRITOS

1. In a small bowl, beat the eggs and egg whites with the salt and pepper.
2. In a small nonstick skillet, heat the olive oil over medium heat. Add the spinach and sauté briefly, until just wilted.
3. Pour the eggs into the pan and scramble, stirring regularly, until cooked through, 3 to 4 minutes.
4. Add one-quarter of the egg mixture to each tortilla and sprinkle each with 1 tablespoon of cheese. If using, add a few avocado slices on top of the egg mixture. Fold the two sides in, then roll up the burrito. Serve with the salsa.

Tip: In the spring, when fresh greens are abundant, consider swapping out the spinach for a spicier green, such as arugula or watercress, for a bolder flavor.

Per Serving: Calories: 332; Protein: 27g; Total carbs: 28g; Fiber: 7g; Fat: 12g

Open-Faced Breakfast Tacos

SERVINGS: 2 / PREP TIME: 10 MINUTES / COOK TIME: 20 MINUTES

Quick, protein-packed, and endlessly customizable, these breakfast tacos are a go-to for busy mornings when you still want to eat with intention. They deliver a satisfying mix of flavor and fullness that helps keep cravings in check. Use what you have on hand, boost the protein, spice it up: This one is all about flexibility that works for your goals.

Nonstick cooking spray
1 cup cooked or canned black beans, rinsed and drained
½ cup chopped tomato
½ cup chopped green bell pepper
4 tablespoons chopped red onion, divided
1 teaspoon minced jalapeño pepper
Juice of 1 lime
1 teaspoon extra virgin olive oil
4 organic corn tortillas
4 large eggs
Freshly ground black pepper
2 tablespoons chopped fresh cilantro
Dash hot sauce (optional, not included in nutrition information)
Avocado slices (optional, not included in nutrition information)

1. Preheat the oven to 350°F. Lightly coat a baking sheet with nonstick cooking spray.
2. In a small bowl, toss together the beans, tomato, bell pepper, 2 tablespoons of red onion, the jalapeño, lime juice, and oil.
3. Lay out the tortillas on the prepared baking sheet. Spoon an equal portion of the bean mixture on each tortilla. Create a shallow "nest" in the mixture on each tortilla and crack an egg into it. Sprinkle each egg with pepper.
4. Bake for 15 to 17 minutes, depending on how well you like the egg yolk to be cooked.
5. Top with the remaining 2 tablespoons of chopped onions and the cilantro. Add hot sauce or avocado (if using).

Per Serving: Calories: 417; Protein: 25g; Total carbs: 51g; Fiber: 11g; Fat: 14g

Crispy Classic Chilaquiles

SERVINGS: 2 / PREP TIME: 10 MINUTES / COOK TIME: 20 MINUTES

This bold, veggie-filled breakfast brings serious flavor and serious staying power. Chilaquiles are a great way to start your day with fiber, color, and warmth, and when you top them with an egg (or two), you turn them into a high-protein meal that actually keeps you full. It's the kind of comfort food that fits perfectly into your fat-loss or maintenance phase without feeling restrictive.

- 6 organic corn tortillas
- 1½ tablespoons extra virgin olive oil, divided
- Freshly ground black pepper
- 4 medium tomatoes, sliced
- 4 tablespoons diced green chiles
- 4 garlic cloves, peeled
- 1 cup diced onion
- 1 cup shredded cooked chicken
- ½ cup chopped fresh cilantro
- Avocado slices (optional, not included in nutrition information)
- 2 tablespoons grated parmesan cheese (optional, not included in nutrition information)
- 2 tablespoons minced jalapeños (optional, not included in nutrition information)

1. Preheat the oven to 350°F. Line a baking sheet with aluminum foil.
2. Slice the tortillas into 1-inch strips, then slice in the opposite direction to make bite-size pieces.
3. Put the tortilla pieces on the lined baking sheet. Drizzle with half of the olive oil and toss to blend evenly. Arrange the tortillas in a single layer and lightly sprinkle with pepper. Bake until the tortillas are crisp, 12 to 13 minutes.
4. While the tortillas are baking, add the tomatoes, chiles, and garlic cloves to a food processor and blend until smooth, 20 to 30 seconds.
5. In a medium skillet, heat the remaining olive oil. Add the onion and sauté until slightly browned, 2 to 3 minutes.
6. Add the tomato mixture to the skillet, reduce the heat to medium-low, and simmer until the mixture thickens slightly, 2 to 3 minutes.
7. Add the tortilla strips and shredded chicken, and stir to mix well. Cook until all the ingredients are warmed through, 2 minutes or so. Remove from heat.
8. Divide the chilaquiles between two bowls. Top each portion with cilantro, avocado, parmesan cheese, and jalapeños (if using).

Per Serving: Calories: 469; Protein: 31g; Total carbs: 57g; Fiber: 11g; Fat: 13g

Sweet Potato, Onion, and Turkey Sausage Hash

SERVINGS: 4 / PREP TIME: 10 MINUTES / COOK TIME: 25 MINUTES

This hearty, fiber-rich hash keeps your metabolism humming and your hunger in check. Sweet potatoes offer slow-burning energy and turkey sausage adds the protein your body needs to preserve lean muscle. Top them with an egg, and you've got a balanced, nutrient-dense plate that fuels fat loss and helps you stay full for hours.

- 1 tablespoon extra virgin olive oil
- 2 medium sweet potatoes, cut into ½-inch dice
- 1 pound chicken or turkey breakfast sausage
- 1 small onion, chopped
- ½ red bell pepper, seeded and chopped
- 2 garlic cloves, minced
- Chopped fresh parsley, for garnish

1. In a large skillet, heat the oil over medium-high heat. Add the sweet potatoes and cook, stirring occasionally, for 12 to 15 minutes, until they brown and begin to soften.
2. Add the sausage, onion, bell pepper, and garlic. Cook for 5 to 6 minutes, until the sausage is cooked through and the vegetables soften.
3. Garnish with parsley and serve warm.

Per Serving: Calories: 326; Protein: 24g; Total carbs: 18g; Fiber: 6g; Fat: 18g

Spinach, Artichoke, and Goat Cheese Breakfast Bake

SERVINGS: 4 / PREP TIME: 15 MINUTES / COOK TIME: 35 MINUTES

This one-dish breakfast is a lifesaver for busy mornings. Prep it once and enjoy a high-protein, fiber-filled meal all week long. Artichokes bring prebiotic power, spinach adds a leafy green boost, and goat cheese keeps things creamy and satisfying. It's the kind of meal that fits effortlessly into your plan.

Nonstick cooking spray
1 (10-ounce) package frozen spinach, thawed and drained
1 (14-ounce) can artichoke hearts, drained
¼ cup finely chopped red bell pepper
2 garlic cloves, minced
8 eggs, lightly beaten
1 cup egg whites
¼ cup unsweetened plain almond milk
½ teaspoon salt
½ teaspoon freshly ground black pepper
½ cup crumbled goat cheese

1. Preheat the oven to 375°F.
2. Spray an 8-by-8-inch baking dish with nonstick cooking spray.
3. In a large mixing bowl, combine the spinach, artichoke hearts, bell pepper, garlic, eggs, egg whites, almond milk, salt, and pepper. Stir well to combine.
4. Transfer the mixture to the baking dish. Sprinkle with the goat cheese.
5. Bake for 35 minutes until the eggs are set. Serve warm.

Option tip: Spice things up for breakfast by adding a scant teaspoon of red pepper flakes to this dish.

Per Serving: Calories: 321; Protein: 29g; Total carbs: 11g; Fiber: 5g; Fat: 17g

Brussels Sprout Hash and Eggs

SERVINGS: 2 / PREP TIME: 15 MINUTES / COOK TIME: 20 MINUTES

This simple, savory hash is full of fiber and flavor, and it pairs perfectly with eggs for a protein-packed breakfast that satisfies. Brussels sprouts are a powerhouse veggie for gut health and blood-sugar control, and the lemon-garlic combo brings them to life. Make a double batch and set yourself up for an easy, metabolism-boosting morning all week long.

3 teaspoons extra virgin olive oil, divided
1 pound Brussels sprouts, sliced
2 garlic cloves, thinly sliced
¼ teaspoon salt
Juice of 1 lemon
4 eggs
½ cup egg whites

1. In a large skillet, heat 1½ teaspoons of oil over medium heat.
2. Add the Brussels sprouts and toss. Cook, stirring regularly, for 6 to 8 minutes until browned and softened.
3. Add the garlic and continue to cook until fragrant, about 1 minute.
4. Season with the salt and lemon juice. Transfer to a serving dish and set aside.
5. In the same pan, heat the remaining 1½ teaspoons of oil over medium-high heat.
6. Crack the eggs into a bowl and add the egg whites.
7. Pour the eggs into pan. Fry for 2 to 4 minutes, flip, and continue cooking to desired doneness. Serve the fried eggs over the bed of hash.

Make-ahead tip: Brussels sprouts, like other brassica vegetables, are easy to prep in advance and hold up well both raw and cooked. Prep the Brussels sprouts up to 5 days in advance by slicing them when you have a free moment. Refrigerate in an airtight container until ready for use.

Per Serving: Calories: 372; Protein: 27g; Total carbs: 16g; Fiber: 5g; Fat: 23g

Crispy Breakfast Pita with Egg and Canadian Bacon

SERVINGS: 2 / PREP TIME: 10 MINUTES / COOK TIME: 20 MINUTES

This high-protein, perfectly balanced breakfast feels a little fancy but comes together fast, even on a busy morning. With a crispy base, savory toppings, and a handful of microgreens for extra nutrients, it checks all the boxes: real food, satisfying portions, and lasting energy. It's one of those meals you'll want on repeat, whether you're in fat loss mode or working to maintain.

1 (6-inch) whole grain pita bread
3 teaspoons extra virgin olive oil, divided
2 eggs
1 cup egg whites
2 slices Canadian bacon
Juice of ½ lemon
1 cup microgreens
2 tablespoons crumbled goat cheese
Freshly ground black pepper

1. Heat a large skillet over medium heat.
2. Split the pita bread. Brush each side of each half with ¼ teaspoon of olive oil (using a total of 1 teaspoon oil). Cook for 2 to 3 minutes on each side, then remove the pita halves from the skillet.
3. In the same skillet, heat 1 teaspoon of oil over medium heat.
4. Crack the eggs into a bowl and add the egg whites. Pour the eggs into the skillet and cook until the eggs are set, 2 to 3 minutes. Remove them from the skillet.
5. In the same skillet, cook the Canadian bacon for 3 to 5 minutes, flipping once.
6. In a large bowl, whisk together the remaining 1 teaspoon of oil and the lemon juice. Add the microgreens and toss to combine.
7. Top each pita half with half of the microgreens, 1 piece of bacon, egg, and 1 tablespoon of goat cheese. Season with pepper and serve.

Per Serving: Calories: 352; Protein: 30g; Total carbs: 25g; Fiber: 4g; Fat: 16g

Cherry Berry Breakfast Smoothie

SERVINGS: 1 / PREP TIME: 10 MINUTES

This is a go-to breakfast for busy mornings when you need something fast and filling. Tart cherries and berries bring antioxidants and fiber, greens add a nutrient punch, and the combo of protein powder and healthy fats keeps you full and energized for hours. It's simple, satisfying, and perfectly aligned with your goals.

- ½ cup frozen unsweetened pitted red tart cherries
- ½ cup frozen blueberries or raspberries (or a combination)
- ¼ cup frozen spinach or kale
- ½ cup unsweetened almond milk
- ¼ cup store-bought protein powder
- ¼ cup tart cherry juice
- 1 tablespoon agave nectar or honey
- 1 teaspoon coconut oil
- ½ teaspoon ground cinnamon

In a blender, combine the cherries, berries, spinach or kale, milk, protein powder, cherry juice, agave nectar or honey, oil, and cinnamon. Cover and blend for about 45 seconds, until smooth.

Per Serving: Calories: 322; Protein: 35g; Total carbs: 30g; Fiber: 9g; Fat: 8g

Tropical Coconut Yogurt Chia Bowls

SERVINGS: 2 / PREP TIME: 10 MINUTES, PLUS OVERNIGHT TO CHILL

This creamy, fiber-rich bowl is the kind of slow-digesting breakfast that helps stabilize blood sugar and curb cravings all morning. Chia seeds deliver omega-3s and fiber, while the coconut milk yogurt adds a satisfying creaminess. Top with fruit, nuts, or whatever you have on hand. This one's endlessly adaptable and totally GLP-1 friendly.

2 cups coconut milk yogurt
½ cup unsweetened coconut milk
1 scoop store-bought protein powder
2 tablespoons chia seeds
2 tablespoons unsweetened coconut flakes
1 tablespoon sesame seeds
1 banana, sliced
½ cup diced pineapple, fresh or dried
½ cup diced mango, fresh or dried

1. Put the coconut milk yogurt, coconut milk, protein powder, and chia seeds in a medium glass mixing bowl. Whisk to combine thoroughly. Cover and refrigerate overnight.
2. Toast the coconut flakes and sesame seeds separately in a small dry skillet over medium-low heat, tossing frequently to avoid burning, until golden brown.
3. When ready to serve, transfer the yogurt mixture to individual serving bowls.
4. Arrange the banana, pineapple, and mango on top. Sprinkle with the coconut flakes and sesame seeds.

Substitution tip: If you can't find coconut milk yogurt, use full-fat or low-fat Greek yogurt instead.

Per Serving: Calories: 313; Protein: 16g; Total carbs: 26g; Fiber: 8g; Fat: 18g

CHAPTER 5

Salads and Soups

Chicken Tortilla Soup

SERVINGS: 4 / PREP TIME: 10 MINUTES / COOK TIME: 35 MINUTES

This lighter take on a classic brings all the bold, comforting flavors you'd expect. Lean chicken breast delivers protein to keep you full, and baked tortilla strips add crunch without the grease. It's a satisfying soup you can whip up with minimal effort and pair with a simple salad for a complete, goal-supporting meal.

- 1 tablespoon extra virgin olive oil
- 1 onion, thinly sliced
- 1 garlic clove, minced
- 1 jalapeño pepper, diced
- 1½ pounds boneless, skinless chicken breasts
- 4 cups reduced-sodium chicken broth
- 1 Roma tomato, diced
- ½ teaspoon salt
- 2 (6-inch) corn tortillas, cut into thin strips
- Nonstick cooking spray
- Juice of 1 lime
- Minced fresh cilantro, for garnish
- ¼ cup shredded Cheddar cheese, for garnish

1. In a medium pot, heat the oil over medium-high heat. Add the onion and cook for 3 to 5 minutes until it begins to soften.
2. Add the garlic and jalapeño and cook until fragrant, about 1 minute more.
3. Add the chicken, chicken broth, tomato, and salt to the pot and bring to a boil. Reduce the heat to medium and simmer gently for 20 to 25 minutes, until the chicken breasts are cooked through. Remove the chicken from the pot and set aside.
4. Preheat the broiler to high.
5. Spray the tortilla strips with nonstick cooking spray and toss to coat. Spread them in a single layer on a baking sheet and broil for 3 to 5 minutes, flipping once, until crisp.
6. When the chicken is cool enough to handle, shred it with two forks and return it to the pot.
7. Season the soup with the lime juice. Serve hot, garnished with cilantro, cheese, and the tortilla strips.

Per Serving: Calories: 305; Protein: 39g; Total carbs: 11g; Fiber: 2g; Fat: 11g

Steak Fajitas with Avocado Salad

SERVINGS: 8 / PREP TIME: 15 MINUTES, PLUS 1 HOUR TO MARINATE / COOK TIME: 15 MINUTES

Lean flank steak provides muscle-supporting protein, while the avocado salad adds fiber and heart-healthy fats to help keep hunger and cravings in check.

FOR THE FLANK STEAK

Juice of 3 limes
2 tablespoons extra virgin olive oil
1 teaspoon ground cumin
1 jalapeño pepper, seeded and roughly chopped
¼ cup chopped fresh cilantro leaves and stems
1 (1½- to 2-pound) flank steak
1 teaspoon organic canola oil

FOR THE AVOCADO SALAD

2 tablespoons extra virgin olive oil
2 tablespoons freshly squeezed lemon juice
½ teaspoon salt
¼ teaspoon freshly ground black pepper
2 tablespoons chopped fresh cilantro leaves
2 ripe avocados, pitted, peeled, and thinly sliced
1 bunch red radishes, thinly sliced

FOR THE FAJITAS

8 whole wheat flour tortillas
Fresh cilantro leaves, for garnish
2 limes, cut into wedges, for garnish

TO MAKE THE FLANK STEAK

1. In a large bowl, combine the lime juice, olive oil, cumin, jalapeño, and cilantro. Mix well. Add the steak and flip it so that the meat is coated all over in the marinade.
2. Cover and refrigerate for at least 1 hour or up to 10 hours.
3. Remove the steak from the marinade, shaking off any excess.
4. Heat a cast-iron pan over medium-high heat for 2 minutes. Pour in the canola oil.
5. When the oil is hot, cook the steak for 3 to 5 minutes per side, depending on desired doneness (3 minutes will yield a medium-rare steak, while 5 will yield a medium to well-done steak).
6. Transfer the steak to a plate and tent with aluminum foil for 5 minutes. Slice the steak thinly against the grain.

TO MAKE THE AVOCADO SALAD

1. In a mixing bowl, whisk together the olive oil, lemon juice, salt, and pepper.
2. Add the cilantro, avocados, and radishes and toss to coat.

TO ASSEMBLE THE FAJITAS

1. Arrange a scoop of the avocado salad on each tortilla and top with a few slices of steak.
2. Garnish with the cilantro and lime wedges and serve.

Per Serving: Calories: 383; Protein: 20g; Total carbs: 24g; Fiber: 6g; Fat: 23g

Ginger-Chicken Noodle Soup

SERVINGS: 4 / PREP TIME: 10 MINUTES / COOK TIME: 20 MINUTES

This cozy bowl takes the comfort of classic chicken noodle soup and gives it a twist. Ginger soothes digestion and adds a warming kick, while boneless chicken thighs bring flavor and protein to keep you full. It's the kind of simple meal that works whether you're easing into a rest day or just need something warm and grounding.

- 1 teaspoon organic canola oil
- 1 pound boneless, skinless chicken thighs, trimmed and cut into bite-size pieces
- 2 carrots, peeled and julienned
- 2 celery stalks, diced
- 4 scallions, thinly sliced (green and white parts)
- 2 garlic cloves, minced
- 4 cups reduced-sodium chicken broth
- 1 cup water
- 1 tablespoon reduced-sodium soy sauce
- 1-inch knob fresh ginger, peeled and grated
- 1½ cups shirataki noodles, drained (see Tip)

1. In a large Dutch oven, heat the oil over medium-high heat. Add the chicken pieces and cook, stirring frequently, until browned.
2. Add the carrots, celery, and scallions, and continue to cook for 2 minutes, stirring regularly. Add the garlic and cook for 1 additional minute.
3. Add the chicken broth, water, soy sauce, and ginger. Cook for 10 minutes to let the flavors meld.
4. Add the noodles and cook until heated through. Serve hot.

Tip: Shirataki noodles are made from the konjac yam and come in a variety of sizes. These low-carbohydrate noodles are high in fiber and low in calories, making them a great option for soups and stews. Find shirataki noodles at well-stocked grocery stores, health food stores, Asian markets, or online. If you need to make a substitution, a thick-cut, linguine-style noodle works best.

Per Serving: Calories: 256; Protein: 24g; Total carbs: 7g; Fiber: 1g; Fat: 14g

Thai-Style Beef Curry

SERVINGS: 4 / PREP TIME: 20 MINUTES / COOK TIME: 10 MINUTES

This rich, comforting curry is packed with bold flavor and high-quality protein, perfect for a satisfying dinner that keeps you full and on track. Use light coconut milk to keep it lighter without losing creaminess, and lean beef to support your muscle and metabolism. Whether you make the curry paste from scratch or grab a store-bought version, this dish proves healthy meals don't have to be boring.

FOR THE CURRY PASTE

1 shallot

1 stalk lemongrass, outer layer and woody upper area discarded, cut into 1-inch sections

1 Thai red chile, stemmed and seeded

4 garlic cloves, peeled

2-inch knob ginger, peeled and sliced

2 tablespoons freshly squeezed lime juice

1 tablespoon fish sauce

1 teaspoon shrimp paste

1 teaspoon ground cumin

1 teaspoon ground coriander

¼ teaspoon ground white pepper

TO MAKE THE CURRY PASTE

Combine the shallot, lemongrass, chile, garlic, ginger, lime juice, fish sauce, shrimp paste, cumin, coriander, and pepper in a food processor. Pulse until coarsely ground. Add a tablespoon or two of water and continue pulsing to form a smooth paste.

Continued on next page >>

FOR THE CURRY

1 (14-ounce) can light coconut milk, divided
1 pound flank steak, thinly sliced against the grain
3 garlic cloves, minced
1 teaspoon grated fresh ginger
½ medium onion, diced
1 red bell pepper, seeded and sliced
1 head broccoli, broken into florets
2 teaspoons fish sauce, plus more if desired
1 teaspoon sugar (optional)
¼ cup chopped fresh cilantro

TO MAKE THE CURRY

1. Heat a large wok over medium-high heat. Transfer the curry paste to the wok, along with 2 to 3 tablespoons of the coconut milk. Cook, stirring constantly, until fragrant, about 1 minute.
2. Add the flank steak and cook, stirring constantly, until it is well browned. Use a spatula to push the steak to the side of the wok, away from the direct heat.
3. Add the garlic and ginger and stir-fry until fragrant. Add the onion, bell pepper, and broccoli and stir to mix. Push the steak back into the middle of the wok and add the remaining coconut milk.
4. Bring the liquid to a simmer and continue to cook until the vegetables are fork-tender, about 10 minutes. Remove from the heat and stir in the fish sauce.
5. Taste and adjust the seasoning, adding the sugar (if using) and more fish sauce according to your preference. Garnish with the cilantro.

Tip: If you choose to use a premade curry paste, start with just 1 tablespoon of the paste and, if desired, add more later on. Commercially prepared curry pastes are typically much hotter than this one, so you'll need less for this recipe.

Per Serving: Calories: 298; Protein: 24g; Total carbs: 13g; Fiber: 3g; Fat: 17g

Chicken Salad with Summer Strawberries and Arugula

SERVINGS: 4 / PREP TIME: 15 MINUTES / COOK TIME: 35 MINUTES

This vibrant salad is summer on a plate. It's fresh, light, and packed with flavor. Juicy strawberries and peppery arugula pair beautifully with lean grilled chicken for a high-protein meal that's as satisfying as it is seasonal. It's a perfect example of how real food can be both nourishing and refreshing, especially when you're eating to feel your best.

1 pound cooked chicken, diced
1 cup chopped celery
½ cup Greek yogurt
Salt
Pepper
½ cup raw almonds
2 teaspoons extra virgin olive oil, divided
1 tablespoon dried rosemary
Pinch cayenne pepper
4 cups arugula
4 large fresh basil leaves, chopped
1 cup sliced fresh strawberries, plus 1 mashed strawberry
½ cup sliced cucumbers
¼ cup avocado cubes
½ cup chopped carrots
3 teaspoons balsamic vinegar
1 teaspoon poppy seeds

1. In a bowl combine the chicken, celery, and yogurt. Season to taste with salt and pepper. Set aside.
2. Preheat the oven to 325°F. Line a baking sheet with parchment paper.
3. On the baking sheet, toss the almonds with 1 teaspoon of olive oil, the rosemary, and the cayenne pepper. Bake for 20 minutes, tossing once to make sure the almonds are evenly coated.
4. In a large bowl, combine the arugula, basil, sliced strawberries, cucumbers, avocado, and carrots.
5. In a small bowl, whisk together the balsamic vinegar, remaining 1 teaspoon of olive oil, poppy seeds, and mashed strawberry. Add the dressing to the arugula blend and mix well.
6. Once the almonds are finished, let them cool for 10 minutes before adding to the top of the salad. Serve with a scoop of chicken salad on the side.

Tip: Berries such as the strawberries found in this recipe are the best types of fruits for those with diabetes, as they are low on the glycemic index yet high in satisfying fiber.

Per Serving: Calories: 383; Protein: 43g; Total carbs: 13g; Fiber: 5g; Fat: 17g

Lemon-Garlic Shrimp Skewers over Caesar Salad

SERVINGS: 4 / PREP TIME: 15 MINUTES, PLUS 10 MINUTES TO MARINATE / COOK TIME: 10 MINUTES

This fresh, high-protein meal delivers everything you want in a Caesar, with crisp greens, creamy dressing, and bold flavor, all without the additives of store-bought versions. The yogurt-based dressing is light yet satisfying, and the marinated shrimp skewers add lean protein to keep you full and fueled. Don't skip the anchovies; they melt right in and bring classic umami punch without the fishiness.

FOR THE CROUTONS

4 slices high-fiber whole grain bread
1 large garlic clove, peeled and halved
1 teaspoon extra virgin olive oil

FOR THE SHRIMP

1 pound large shrimp, peeled and deveined
3 tablespoons freshly squeezed lemon juice
1 tablespoon extra virgin olive oil
3 garlic cloves, minced
½ teaspoon freshly ground black pepper

TO MAKE THE CROUTONS

1. Preheat the oven to 375° F.
2. Rub the cut garlic on each slice of bread, on both sides.
3. Cut the bread into 1-inch squares and toss with olive oil.
4. Bake for 10 to 15 minutes, tossing once halfway through.

TO MAKE THE SHRIMP

1. In a small bowl, toss the shrimp with the lemon juice, olive oil, garlic, and pepper. Mix well and set aside to marinate for 10 minutes.
2. Preheat the broiler to high.
3. Thread the shrimp onto four skewers and place the skewers on a baking sheet.
4. Place the baking sheet under the broiler and broil, flipping once, until the shrimp turn pink, 3 to 5 minutes per side.
5. Remove and set aside.

Continued on next page >>

FOR THE SALAD

¼ cup plain 2% Greek yogurt
1 tablespoon extra virgin olive oil
2 tablespoons freshly squeezed lemon juice
1 teaspoon anchovy paste
½ teaspoon Dijon mustard
2 garlic cloves, peeled
8 cups bite-size pieces romaine lettuce
1 large cucumber, halved lengthwise and thinly sliced crosswise
¼ cup grated parmesan cheese

TO MAKE THE SALAD

1. In a small bowl, whisk together the yogurt, olive oil, lemon juice, anchovy paste, mustard, and garlic.
2. In a large bowl, toss the dressing with the lettuce and cucumber until well coated.
3. Add the croutons and parmesan cheese, and toss again to integrate.
4. Divide the salad among four plates and top each with a shrimp skewer. Serve.

Tip: If using wooden skewers for the shrimp, be sure to soak them in water for 30 minutes before threading. If using metal skewers, oil them lightly before threading.

Per Serving: Calories: 396; Protein: 32g; Total carbs: 28g; Fiber: 5g; Fat 6g

Grilled Chicken with Crisp Cucumber and Lime Salad

SERVINGS: 4 / PREP TIME: 10 MINUTES, PLUS 15 MINUTES TO CHILL / COOK TIME: 10 MINUTES

This bright, refreshing dish is perfect for warm days and laid-back gatherings. Lean grilled chicken keeps it protein-packed, while crunchy jicama, juicy blueberries, and fresh mint bring color and texture. It's light and hydrating, exactly the kind of meal that supports your goals while still feeling fun and celebratory.

1 pound chicken breast
1 tablespoon extra virgin olive oil
Salt
Pepper
½ cup fresh blueberries
1 cup diced cucumber
1 cup diced jicama
4 fresh mint leaves, chopped
Juice of 1 lime

1. Turn a grill on medium-high heat.
2. Brush the chicken with olive oil, then season to taste with salt and pepper. Grill the chicken for 5 to 7 minutes per side. Transfer it to a plate and set aside.
3. In a medium mixing bowl, toss together the blueberries, cucumber, jicama, and mint leaves. Sprinkle the lime juice over the mixture and toss to blend.
4. Refrigerate for at least 15 minutes. Serve the salad alongside the grilled chicken.

Per Serving: Calories: 258; Protein: 34g; Total carbs: 7g; Fiber: 2g; Fat: 10g

Southern Chicken Salad

SERVINGS: 4 / PREP TIME: 10 MINUTES / COOK TIME: 25 MINUTES

This lighter take on a classic Southern comfort food swaps protein-rich Greek yogurt for mayo, giving you all the creaminess with none of the compromise. It's a dish rooted in celebration and nostalgia, but now built to support your goals. Whether you serve it at a gathering or prep it for weekday lunches, it's a feel-good, crowd-pleasing favorite you'll come back to again and again.

- 1 pound boneless, skinless chicken breasts
- ¾ cup chopped spinach
- ½ cup diced celery
- ½ cup red grapes, quartered
- ½ cup plain 2% Greek yogurt
- ¼ cup chopped pecans
- 2 tablespoons dried cherries or raisins
- ½ teaspoon poultry seasoning
- ½ teaspoon salt
- ¼ teaspoon onion powder
- ¼ teaspoon freshly ground black pepper

1. Bring a large pot of water to a boil over medium-high heat. Add the chicken and cook for 25 minutes.
2. With a slotted spoon, transfer the chicken to a large mixing bowl; reserve ¼ cup of the cooking liquid.
3. Once the chicken is cool enough to handle, shred it into small pieces with your fingers. Add the reserved cooking liquid.
4. Add the remaining ingredients and mix to combine. Enjoy!

Tip: Magnesium is a very important mineral for individuals with diabetes because it helps regulate blood sugar. This recipe is rich in magnesium, thanks to the spinach and pecans.

Per Serving: Calories: 225; Protein: 26g; Total carbs: 11g; Fiber: 2g; Fat: 9g

Fiesta Salad with Shrimp

SERVINGS: 4 / PREP TIME: 15 MINUTES

Healthy foods should never be too complicated or time-consuming to prepare, because that would make them difficult to incorporate into your daily routine. This salad provides fiber, protein, slow-digesting carbs, and plenty of nutrients. Serve it as an appetizer, dip, or simple addition to any meal.

- 1 pound cooked shrimp, chopped
- 1 cup cooked or canned black beans, rinsed and drained
- 1 heirloom tomato, chopped
- 1 green bell pepper, seeded and diced
- ½ avocado, diced
- 1 tablespoon minced jalapeño pepper
- Pinch freshly ground black pepper
- Pinch cayenne pepper
- 2 tablespoons chopped fresh cilantro
- Juice of 1 lime

Simply toss together the shrimp, beans, tomato, bell pepper, avocado, jalapeño, pepper, cayenne, cilantro, and lime juice in a bowl and enjoy!

Tip: Tomatoes are a superfood for individuals with diabetes. Many people don't realize that tomatoes are a fantastic source of vitamin C, helping our bodies absorb iron and heal cuts. It also acts as an antioxidant to prevent damage to our bodies' cells.

Per Serving: Calories: 297; Protein: 23g; Total carbs: 24g; Fiber: 8g; Fat: 12g

CHAPTER 6

Fish and Seafood

Tuna, Hummus, and Veggie Wraps

SERVINGS: 4 / PREP TIME: 15 MINUTES

These wraps are a perfect real-food meal that keeps you full, energized, and on track. Tuna brings lean protein, homemade hummus adds fiber and healthy fats, and crunchy veggies add color and texture. Whether you need a quick lunch or a high-protein snack, this wrap fits seamlessly into your day.

FOR THE HUMMUS

1 cup from 1 (15-ounce) can reduced-sodium chickpeas, drained and rinsed
2 tablespoons tahini
1 tablespoon extra virgin olive oil
1 garlic clove
Juice of ½ lemon
¼ teaspoon salt
2 tablespoons water

FOR THE WRAPS

4 large lettuce leaves
2 (5-ounce) cans tuna
1 red bell pepper, seeded and cut into strips
1 cucumber, sliced

TO MAKE THE HUMMUS

In a blender, combine the chickpeas, tahini, olive oil, garlic, lemon juice, salt, and water. Process until smooth. Taste and adjust with additional lemon juice or salt, as needed.

TO MAKE THE WRAPS

1. On each lettuce leaf, spread 1 tablespoon of hummus, and divide the tuna among the leaves.
2. Top each with several strips of red pepper and cucumber slices.
3. Roll up the lettuce leaves, folding in the two shorter sides and rolling away from you, like a burrito. Serve.

Per Serving: Calories: 273; Protein: 21g; Total carbs: 24g; Fiber: 9g; Fat: 1g

Blackened Tilapia with Mango Salsa

SERVINGS: 2 / PREP TIME: 15 MINUTES / COOK TIME: 10 MINUTES

This simple, high-protein meal is light, flavorful, and perfect for warmer days, or anytime you want something quick and satisfying. The tilapia is mild and budget friendly, while the mango salsa adds fiber, color, and a fresh, tropical twist. It's a delicious way to stay on track with your goals while keeping meals exciting and full of real-food ingredients.

FOR THE SALSA

1 cup chopped mango
2 tablespoons chopped red onion
2 tablespoons chopped fresh cilantro
2 tablespoons freshly squeezed lime juice
½ jalapeño pepper, seeded and minced
Pinch salt

FOR THE TILAPIA

1 tablespoon paprika
1 teaspoon onion powder
½ teaspoon freshly ground black pepper
½ teaspoon dried thyme
½ teaspoon garlic powder
¼ teaspoon cayenne pepper
¼ teaspoon salt
1 pound boneless tilapia fillets
2 teaspoons extra virgin olive oil
1 lime, cut into wedges, for serving

TO MAKE THE SALSA

In a medium bowl, toss together the mango, onion, cilantro, lime juice, jalapeño, and salt. Set aside.

TO MAKE THE TILAPIA

1. In a small bowl, mix the paprika, onion powder, pepper, thyme, garlic powder, cayenne, and salt. Rub the mixture on both sides of the tilapia fillets.
2. In a large skillet, heat the oil over medium heat, and cook the fish for 3 to 5 minutes on each side until the outer coating is crisp and the fish is cooked through.
3. Spoon half of the salsa over each fillet and serve with lime wedges on the side.

Substitution tip: Pineapple salsa also pairs well with the heat of this dish. Substitute an equal amount of fresh or canned pineapple for the mango.

Per Serving: Calories: 317; Protein: 46g; Total carbs: 15g; Fiber: 2g; Fat: 9g

Cajun Shrimp Casserole

SERVINGS: 4 / PREP TIME: 15 MINUTES / COOK TIME: 30 MINUTES

Bold flavor meets balanced nutrition in this spicy, cheesy, high-protein casserole. The shrimp is lean protein, quinoa adds fiber and all nine essential amino acids, and the Cajun seasoning gives it that craveable kick. This one-dish meal keeps you full and proves you don't have to sacrifice flavor to stay on track.

½ cup quinoa
1 cup water
1 pound shrimp, peeled and deveined
1½ teaspoons Cajun seasoning, divided
4 tomatoes, diced
1 tablespoon plus 2 teaspoons extra virgin olive oil, divided
½ onion, diced
1 jalapeño pepper, seeded and minced
3 garlic cloves, minced
1 tablespoon tomato paste
¼ teaspoon freshly ground black pepper
½ cup shredded pepper jack cheese

1. In a pot, combine the quinoa and water. Bring to a boil, reduce the heat, cover, and simmer on low for 10 to 15 minutes until all the water is absorbed. Fluff with a fork.
2. Preheat the oven to 350°F.
3. In a large mixing bowl, toss the shrimp with half of the Cajun seasoning.
4. In another bowl, toss the remaining Cajun seasoning with the tomatoes and 1½ teaspoons of olive oil.
5. In a large, oven-safe skillet, heat 1 tablespoon of olive oil over medium heat. Add the shrimp and cook for 2 to 3 minutes per side until they are opaque and firm. Remove the shrimp from the skillet and set aside.
6. In the same skillet, heat the remaining olive oil over medium-high heat. Add the onion, jalapeño, and garlic, and cook until the onion softens, 3 to 5 minutes.
7. Add the seasoned tomatoes, tomato paste, cooked quinoa, and pepper. Stir well to combine.
8. Return the shrimp to the skillet, placing them in a single layer on top of the quinoa. Sprinkle the cheese over the top.
9. Transfer the skillet to the oven and bake for 15 minutes.
10. Preheat the broiler to high, and broil for 2 minutes to brown the cheese. Serve.

Per Serving: Calories: 317; Protein: 30g; Total carbs: 18g; Fiber: 3g; Fat: 14g

Shrimp Burgers with Fruity Salsa and Salad

SERVINGS: 4 / PREP TIME: 15 MINUTES, PLUS 30 MINUTES TO MARINATE / COOK TIME: 10 MINUTES

These juicy, protein-packed shrimp burgers are a fresh twist on a cookout classic. Paired with a bright, fruity salsa and a crisp salad, they deliver the kind of nutrient-dense meal that fuels fat loss.

FOR THE SALSA

1 cup diced mango
1 avocado, diced
1 scallion, both white and green parts, finely chopped
1 tablespoon chopped fresh cilantro
Juice of 1 lime
¼ teaspoon freshly ground black pepper

FOR THE BURGERS

1 pound shrimp, peeled and deveined
1 large egg
½ red bell pepper, seeded and coarsely chopped
¼ cup chopped scallions, both white and green parts
2 tablespoons fresh chopped cilantro
2 garlic cloves
¼ teaspoon freshly ground black pepper
1 tablespoon extra virgin olive oil
4 cups mixed salad greens
4 whole wheat hamburger buns (optional)

TO MAKE THE SALSA

In a small bowl, toss the mango, avocado, scallion, and cilantro. Sprinkle with the lime juice and pepper. Mix gently to combine and set aside.

TO MAKE THE BURGERS

1. In a food processor or blender, add half the shrimp and process until coarsely pureed.
2. Add the egg, bell pepper, scallions, cilantro, and garlic and process until uniformly chopped. Transfer the mixture to a large mixing bowl.
3. Using a sharp knife, chop the remaining half pound of shrimp into small pieces. Add the pieces to the pureed mixture and stir well to combine. Add the pepper and stir well.
4. Form the mixture into 4 patties of equal size. Arrange on a plate, cover, and refrigerate for 30 minutes.
5. In a large skillet, heat the olive oil over medium heat. Cook the burgers for 3 minutes on each side, until browned and cooked through.
6. On each of 4 plates, arrange 1 cup of salad greens and top with a scoop of salsa and a shrimp burger (bun optional).

Per Serving: Calories: 250; Protein: 27g; Total carbs: 13g; Fiber: 3g; Fat: 11g

Tomato Tuna Melts

SERVINGS: 2 / PREP TIME: 5 MINUTES / COOK TIME: 5 MINUTES

These quick, flavor-packed melts are a lunchtime staple that are high in protein, low in effort, and anything but boring. This a smart, satisfying choice whether you're working on fat loss or maintenance. Ready in minutes, these tuna melts are perfect for powering you through your day.

- 1 (3-ounce) can chunk light tuna packed in water, drained
- ½ cup plain nonfat Greek yogurt
- 2 teaspoons freshly squeezed lemon juice
- 2 tablespoons finely chopped celery
- 1 tablespoon finely chopped red onion
- Pinch cayenne pepper
- 1 large tomato, cut into ¾-inch-thick rounds
- ½ cup shredded Cheddar cheese
- 4 slices whole grain bread

1. Preheat the broiler to high.
2. In a medium bowl, combine the tuna, yogurt, lemon juice, celery, red onion, and cayenne pepper. Stir well.
3. Arrange the tomato slices on a baking sheet. Top each with some tuna salad and Cheddar cheese.
4. Broil for 3 to 4 minutes until the cheese is melted and bubbly.
5. While the tomato and tuna cooks, toast the bread.
6. Arrange the tomato and tuna melts across two slices. Place the remaining slices on top to make two sandwiches.

Per Serving: Calories: 435; Protein: 32g; Total carbs: 42g; Fiber: 5g; Fat: 13g

Oven-Baked "Fried" Whitefish

SERVINGS: 4 / PREP TIME: 15 MINUTES / COOK TIME: 25 MINUTES

This lightened-up version of fried fish gives you all the crispy satisfaction without the excess oil. Quinoa breadcrumbs add crunch and fiber, while just a touch of butter helps create that golden finish. It's a great way to enjoy comfort food: perfect for anyone looking to support fat loss or long-term maintenance without missing out.

- 1½ pounds firm whitefish fillets
- 1 tablespoon organic canola oil
- Grated zest and juice of 1 lemon
- 1 teaspoon onion powder
- ½ teaspoon garlic powder
- ½ teaspoon freshly ground black pepper
- ½ cup whole wheat breadcrumbs
- ¼ cup cooked quinoa or additional ¼ cup whole wheat breadcrumbs
- 1 tablespoon unsalted butter, melted

1. Preheat the oven to 425°F. Line a baking sheet with parchment paper.
2. Place the fish on a plate. Drizzle each fillet with oil and lemon juice and sprinkle the lemon zest, onion powder, garlic powder, and pepper on top.
3. Combine the breadcrumbs and quinoa on a plate, and gently roll each fillet in the breadcrumbs, pressing them into the surface. Transfer the fish to the lined baking sheet. Drizzle with the melted butter.
4. Bake until the breadcrumbs are browned and the fish flakes easily, 15 to 20 minutes.

Tip: You can prep these fillets in advance by following the recipe through step 3. When complete, place the baking sheet in the freezer and leave for at least 1 to 3 hours. Pack the frozen fish pieces in a freezer-safe bag or container. When ready to use, bake until cooked through, browned, and crisp, 25 to 30 minutes.

Per Serving: Calories: 275; Protein: 33g; Total carbs: 15g; Fiber: 2g; Fat: 8g

Roasted Salmon with Salsa Verde

SERVINGS: 4 / PREP TIME: 5 MINUTES / COOK TIME: 25 MINUTES

Salmon is a metabolism-supporting powerhouse that is rich in protein and omega-3s that benefit your heart, brain, and mood. This simple recipe highlights everything we love about it: crisp, flavorful salmon paired with a bright, herb-packed salsa verde. Short on time? Store-bought salsa works, too. Add a side of rice or corn tortillas for a well-rounded meal.

Nonstick cooking spray
8 ounces tomatillos, husks removed
½ onion, quartered
1 jalapeño or serrano pepper, seeded
1 garlic clove, unpeeled
1 teaspoon extra virgin olive oil
½ teaspoon salt, divided
4 (4-ounce) wild-caught salmon fillets
¼ teaspoon freshly ground black pepper
¼ cup chopped fresh cilantro
Juice of 1 lime

1. Preheat the oven to 425°F. Spray a baking sheet with non-stick cooking spray.
2. In a large bowl, toss the tomatillos, onion, pepper, garlic, olive oil, and ¼ teaspoon of salt to coat.
3. Arrange the tossed veggies in a single layer on the prepared baking sheet and roast for about 10 minutes, until just softened. Transfer to a dish or plate and set aside.
4. Arrange the salmon fillets skin-side down on the same baking sheet, and season with the remaining ¼ teaspoon of salt and the pepper.
5. Bake for 12 to 15 minutes, until the fish is firm and flakes easily.
6. Meanwhile, peel the roasted garlic and place it and the roasted vegetables in a blender or food processor. Add a scant ¼ cup of water and process until smooth.
7. Add the cilantro and lime juice, and pulse three or four times. Serve the salmon topped with the salsa verde.

Per Serving: Calories: 210; Protein: 21g; Total carbs: 5g; Fiber: 2g; Fat: 13g

Cashew and Parmesan Crusted Salmon

SERVINGS: 4 / PREP TIME: 5 MINUTES / COOK TIME: 15 MINUTES

This flavorful spin on salmon adds a satisfying crunch with a protein-packed crust. Cashews and parmesan bring texture and richness, while the salmon delivers omega-3s to support your heart and brain. It's an easy, nutrient-dense dinner that feels indulgent but works hard for your goals.

- Nonstick cooking spray
- 4 (4- to 6-ounce) wild salmon fillets
- 4 teaspoons extra virgin olive oil
- ¼ cup unsalted cashews
- ¼ cup fresh parsley leaves
- ¼ cup grated parmesan cheese
- 2 garlic cloves, peeled
- ¼ teaspoon freshly ground black pepper
- 4 lemon wedges

1. Preheat the oven to 350°F. Line a baking sheet with aluminum foil and lightly coat the foil with nonstick cooking spray.
2. Rinse the salmon fillets, pat them dry with paper towels, and place them skin-side down on the prepared baking sheet. Brush each salmon fillet with 1 teaspoon of olive oil.
3. Combine the cashews, parsley, parmesan cheese, garlic, and pepper in a food processor. Pulse until the mixture is fine like sand. Spread the mixture evenly over the fillets.
4. Bake for 12 to 13 minutes. Then preheat the broiler to high and broil until the topping is lightly browned, about 2 more minutes.
5. Transfer the fillets to serving plates and squeeze the juice of a lemon wedge over each.

Per Serving: Calories: 374; Protein: 29g; Total carbs: 4g; Fiber: 1g; Fat: 25g

Crab Cakes

SERVINGS: 4 / PREP TIME: 20 MINUTES / COOK TIME: 20 MINUTES

These crispy golden crab cakes are packed with lean protein and bold flavor, perfect for a light lunch or easy weeknight dinner. Leaving the crab in chunks keeps the texture satisfying, while a quick pan sear locks in taste without excess fat. Serve with a simple side salad or veggie slaw for a balanced, metabolism-supporting meal you'll come back to again and again.

- 1 large egg
- ¼ cup egg whites
- ¼ cup plain 2% Greek yogurt
- ¼ cup whole wheat breadcrumbs
- 2 tablespoons chopped fresh parsley
- 1 teaspoon grated lemon zest
- ½ teaspoon freshly ground black pepper
- 1 pound lump crabmeat
- 1 tablespoon extra virgin olive oil
- Lemons, cut into wedges, for serving

1. In a mixing bowl, combine the egg, egg whites, yogurt, breadcrumbs, parsley, lemon zest, and pepper. Mix well.
2. Gently fold in the crabmeat, working to incorporate it without breaking up the large pieces.
3. Shape the mixture into 8 balls and flatten them into patties. Arrange these on a plate and refrigerate for 10 minutes.
4. In a large skillet, heat the olive oil over medium heat. Add the crab cakes to the pan and cook until nicely browned and cooked through, 6 to 7 minutes per side.
5. Remove the patties from the pan and serve hot with the lemon wedges.

Per Serving: Calories: 184; Protein: 25g; Total carbs: 6g; Fiber: 2g; Fat: 6g

Grilled Zucchini with Cinnamon Citrus Cod

SERVINGS: 2 / PREP TIME: 20 MINUTES, PLUS 2 HOURS TO MARINATE / COOK TIME: 25 MINUTES

This light, flavorful dish is a perfect example of how simple ingredients can deliver big nutrition. The cinnamon and citrus bring unexpected warmth to lean, flaky cod, making it a standout protein for your balanced plate. Paired with a grilled zucchini salad, it's carb-conscious, fresh, and ideal for fat loss or maintenance without feeling like a compromise.

FOR THE ZUCCHINI

4 small zucchinis
¼ cup extra virgin olive oil
¼ cup white wine vinegar
1 tablespoon Dijon mustard
½ tablespoon maple syrup
2 garlic cloves, minced
½ teaspoon salt
½ teaspoon freshly ground black pepper
Leaves from 3 fresh mint sprigs, for garnish

FOR THE COD

Nonstick cooking spray
2 (4- to 6-ounce) cod fillets
2 teaspoons extra virgin olive oil
1 tablespoon freshly squeezed lemon juice
½ teaspoon salt
½ teaspoon freshly ground black pepper
½ teaspoon ground cinnamon
½ teaspoon ground cumin
¼ teaspoon freshly grated ginger
¼ teaspoon garlic powder

TO MAKE THE ZUCCHINI

1. Cut the stem end off each zucchini. Cut the zucchini on the bias into thin ovals.
2. In a small bowl, whisk together the olive oil, vinegar, mustard, maple syrup, garlic, salt, and pepper.
3. Pour the marinade over the zucchini. Cover and refrigerate for 2 hours.

TO MAKE THE COD AND SERVE

1. Preheat the oven to 400°F. Lightly coat a baking sheet with nonstick cooking spray.
2. Place the cod on the prepared baking sheet and drizzle each fillet with olive oil and lemon juice. Season each with the salt and pepper.
3. In a small mixing bowl, combine the cinnamon, cumin, ginger, and garlic powder. Sprinkle the mixture evenly over the cod fillets and place the fillets in the oven.
4. Bake until the fish flakes easily, 10 to 12 minutes.
5. Preheat a grill to medium-high.
6. Grill the zucchini slices for 1 to 2 minutes on each side, until just tender. Serve with the baked fish and garnish with the mint.

Per Serving: Calories: 312; Protein: 23g; Total carbs: 11g; Fiber: 2g; Fat: 18g

CHAPTER 7

Poultry and Meat

Skillet Chicken with Asparagus and Quinoa

SERVINGS: 4 / PREP TIME: 10 MINUTES / COOK TIME: 25 MINUTES

This one-pan meal brings together lean protein, fiber-rich quinoa, and vibrant veggies for a balanced plate that supports fat loss and energy. A touch of turmeric adds anti-inflammatory benefits without overpowering the dish. It's comfort food, upgraded.

- 1 pound asparagus, trimmed and cut into 1-inch pieces
- 1 tablespoon plus 1 teaspoon extra virgin olive oil, divided
- ½ teaspoon salt
- ¼ teaspoon freshly ground black pepper
- 1 cup water
- ½ cup quinoa, rinsed and drained
- 1 pound boneless, skinless chicken breasts, cut into 2-inch pieces
- 1 tablespoon ground turmeric
- 2 cups chopped spinach
- 2 tablespoons balsamic vinegar
- ½ teaspoon garlic powder
- ¼ cup feta cheese (optional)

1. Preheat the oven to 400°F. Line a baking sheet with parchment paper.
2. Spread out the asparagus on the baking sheet and toss with 1 teaspoon of olive oil. Season with the salt and pepper.
3. Bake for 10 minutes, stirring once.
4. Meanwhile, in a small saucepan, bring the water to a boil. Add the quinoa, reduce the heat to low, and cover for 15 minutes. The quinoa is done when all the water is evaporated. Fluff with a fork and set aside.
5. While the quinoa is cooking, heat the remaining oil in a large skillet over medium-high heat. Add the chicken and turmeric. Sauté until cooked through, 4 to 5 minutes.
6. Add the cooked asparagus, chopped spinach, chicken, balsamic vinegar, and garlic powder to the quinoa and stir to combine.
7. Sprinkle the feta cheese on top (if using). Serve warm.

Tip: Studies have shown that the curcumin found in turmeric has anti-inflammatory properties. Piperine, a compound found in black pepper, can help increase this effect.

Per Serving: Calories: 286; Protein: 32g; Total carbs: 23g; Fiber: 5g; Fat: 9g

Classic Chicken Comfort Bowl

SERVINGS: 4 / PREP TIME: 5 MINUTES / COOK TIME: 4 TO 6 HOURS

This slow-cooked staple is everything a high-protein meal should be: simple to prep, easy to love, and endlessly versatile. It's packed with flavor and keeps you full, making it ideal for busy weeks when you still want to eat with purpose. Double the batch and use the leftovers in tacos, salads, or wraps.

- 1 pound boneless, skinless chicken breasts
- ½ cup salsa
- 1⅓ cups cooked brown rice
- 2 cups cooked or canned black beans, rinsed and drained
- 1 cup cherry tomatoes, quartered
- ¼ cup chopped red onion
- 4 cups chopped romaine lettuce
- 1 avocado, pitted, peeled, and sliced
- ¼ cup chopped fresh cilantro
- 4 lime wedges

1. Put the chicken in the slow cooker and pour the salsa over it. Cover and cook on low for 4 to 6 hours.
2. Shred the chicken.
3. Distribute the chicken, salsa, rice, beans, tomatoes, onion, lettuce, avocado, and cilantro evenly among four bowls. Squeeze the juice of 1 lime wedge over each bowl and serve.

Per Serving: Calories: 397; Protein: 37g; Total carbs: 44g; Fiber: 11g; Fat: 9g

Chipotle Chicken with Creamy Avocado-Lime Sauce

SERVINGS: 4 / PREP TIME: 15 MINUTES, PLUS 30 MINUTES TO MARINATE / COOK TIME: 35 MINUTES

Spicy, satisfying, and packed with protein, this dish proves that real food can be both bold and balanced. The avocado-lime sauce is rich in healthy fats and so versatile you'll want to drizzle it on everything.

FOR THE CHICKEN

1½ pounds boneless, skinless chicken breast
2 tablespoons extra virgin olive oil
1½ tablespoons lime juice
1 teaspoon maple syrup
½ teaspoon chipotle chile powder
½ teaspoon garlic powder
Pinch salt
Pinch freshly ground black pepper

FOR THE CREAMY LIME SAUCE

½ ripe avocado
1 tablespoon chopped seeded jalapeño pepper
1 garlic clove, peeled
1 tablespoon extra virgin olive oil
¼ teaspoon grated lime zest
1½ tablespoons lime juice
2 tablespoons chopped fresh cilantro
Pinch salt
Pinch freshly ground black pepper

TO MAKE THE CHICKEN

1. Put the chicken in a zip-top bag.
2. In a small bowl, whisk together the olive oil, lime juice, maple syrup, chipotle chile powder, garlic powder, salt, and pepper. Add the marinade to the bag with the chicken, seal it, and toss a few times to make sure the marinade is distributed over all the chicken. Refrigerate for at least 30 minutes.
3. Preheat the oven to 400°F.
4. Remove the chicken from the marinade and transfer it to in an 8-inch-square baking dish. Bake until a thermometer inserted in a breast reads 165°F, 30 to 35 minutes.

TO MAKE THE CREAMY LIME SAUCE

1. While the chicken is cooking, prepare the creamy lime sauce by combining all the ingredients in a food processor and processing until smooth.
2. Top each serving of the chicken with 1 to 2 tablespoons of the creamy sauce.

Per Serving: Calories: 321; Protein: 40g; Total carbs: 5g; Fiber: 2g; Fat: 22g

Creamy Broccoli and Chicken Casserole

SERVINGS: 4 / PREP TIME: 20 MINUTES / COOK TIME: 35 MINUTES

This cozy one-dish meal is everything you want at the end of a long day: warm, filling, and packed with protein. Ditching the canned soup for a simple homemade sauce keeps it real-food focused without adding preparation time.

- Nonstick cooking spray
- 1 cup cooked quinoa (prepared with low-sodium chicken broth instead of water)
- 1 (16-ounce) bag frozen (thawed) broccoli or 2 cups fresh broccoli florets
- 2½ cups diced cooked chicken
- 2 cups unsweetened almond milk
- ¼ cup whole wheat flour
- ¼ cup plain nonfat Greek yogurt
- ½ cup grated sharp Cheddar cheese
- 1 teaspoon garlic powder
- ¼ teaspoon salt
- ½ teaspoon freshly ground black pepper
- Dash cayenne pepper
- 2 tablespoons walnuts
- 2 tablespoons grated parmesan cheese
- 2 tablespoons whole wheat breadcrumbs
- 1 tablespoon extra virgin olive oil

1. Preheat the oven to 375°F.
2. Coat an 8-inch-square baking dish with nonstick cooking spray. Spread out the quinoa in the baking dish and cover it with the broccoli and chicken.
3. In a medium saucepan set over medium-high heat, whisk together the almond milk and whole wheat flour until slightly thickened, about 5 minutes.
4. Add the Greek yogurt, Cheddar cheese, garlic powder, salt, black pepper, and cayenne pepper. Stir until everything is melted and combined, 1 to 2 minutes. Pour the mixture over the broccoli, chicken, and quinoa.
5. Combine the walnuts, parmesan cheese, and breadcrumbs in a food processor. Pulse 10 to 20 times, until a fine mixture is made. Transfer the puree to a mixing bowl.
6. Add the olive oil to the puree and mix with your hands to create a crumble. Spread the crumble evenly over the broccoli mixture.
7. Bake for 30 minutes, then serve.

Per Serving: Calories: 398; Protein: 28g; Total carbs: 23g; Fiber: 4g; Fat: 22g

Old-Fashioned Turkey Meatloaf with Sweet Tomato Sauce

SERVINGS: 4 / PREP TIME: 15 MINUTES / COOK TIME: 30 MINUTES

This lighter take on a classic brings all the cozy, nostalgic flavors without weighing you down. Made with lean turkey and a naturally sweet tomato glaze, it's high in protein and perfect for meal prep. The best part? It's endlessly adaptable. Tweak the spices, add your favorite veggies, and make it your own while staying true to your goals.

Nonstick cooking spray
1½ pounds lean ground turkey
3 scallions, chopped
1 cup diced red pepper
1 cup chopped onion
1 large egg
¼ cup egg whites
4 garlic cloves, minced
½ cup whole wheat breadcrumbs
½ cup almond flour
1 tablespoon Italian seasoning
½ teaspoon onion powder
½ teaspoon pepper
½ teaspoon salt
Pinch cayenne
1 medium tomato, sliced
1 date, pitted
2 teaspoons Worcestershire sauce
1 teaspoon chili powder

1. Preheat the oven to 350°F. Lightly coat an 8-inch square baking dish with nonstick cooking spray.
2. In a large mixing bowl, combine the turkey, scallions, pepper, onion, egg, egg whites, garlic, breadcrumbs, flour, Italian seasoning, onion powder, pepper, salt, and cayenne pepper. Mix well with your hands until the ingredients are well combined. Press the meatloaf mixture into the prepared baking dish.
3. Bake until a thermometer inserted in the middle reads 160°F, 25 to 30 minutes.
4. While the meatloaf is cooking, combine the tomato, date, Worcestershire sauce, and chili powder in a food processor and blend until smooth.
5. Transfer the tomato mixture to a saucepan and cook over medium heat until it becomes slightly thickened (the consistency of a smoothie), 10 to 12 minutes.
6. Spread the tomato mixture over the meatloaf for the last 5 to 10 minutes of cooking time.
7. Remove from the oven and cut into 4 slices. Serve.

Per Serving: Calories: 398; Protein: 32g; Total carbs: 23g; Fiber: 5g; Fat: 20g

Sweet-and-Sour Pork and Veggie Stir-Fry

SERVINGS: 6 / PREP TIME: 10 MINUTES, PLUS 30 MINUTES TO MARINATE / COOK TIME: 10 MINUTES

This fast, flavor-packed stir-fry gives you all the sweet-and-savory satisfaction of takeout without the excess sugar, salt, or fat. Lean pork loin and colorful veggies come together in a balanced, high-protein meal that keeps cravings low.

FOR THE PORK

2 tablespoons rice wine or sake
½ teaspoon salt
1 tablespoon cornstarch
1½ pounds pork loin, sliced ¼ inch thick
2 tablespoons canola or vegetable oil

TO MAKE THE PORK

1. In a large bowl, mix the rice wine, salt, and cornstarch. Add the pork loin and toss to combine. Set aside for 30 minutes.
2. In a large wok, heat 1 tablespoon oil over medium-high heat. In batches, pan-fry the pork slices until just starting to brown, about 1 minute per side. (They will not be cooked through.) Use a slotted spoon to transfer the pork to a plate.
3. Once you've finished cooking all the pork, wipe the wok clean with a paper towel.

Continued on next page >>

FOR THE STIR-FRY

½ cup canned pineapple chunks
¼ cup canned pineapple juice
3 tablespoons rice vinegar
1 teaspoon toasted sesame oil
1 teaspoon cornstarch
2 teaspoons organic canola oil
1 red bell pepper, seeded and sliced
1 green bell pepper, seeded and sliced
1 onion, sliced
10 ounces sliced button mushrooms
2 cups cooked rice, for serving (optional)

TO MAKE THE STIR-FRY

1. In a small bowl, combine the pineapple chunks, juice, vinegar, sesame oil, and cornstarch. Set aside.
2. Heat the canola oil in the wok over medium-high heat. Add the peppers and onion to the pan. Cook for 1 minute, stirring constantly. Add the mushrooms and cook for 1 additional minute.
3. Return the pork to the wok and continue to cook until brown spots begin to appear on the meat, 1 to 2 minutes.
4. Using a spatula, push all the meat and vegetables to the sides of the wok. Add the pineapple mixture to the center and bring to a boil. Cook until the sauce begins to thicken, about 1 minute.
5. Stir the meat and vegetables into the sauce to coat. Serve over rice, if desired.

Pro tip: Slice the pork while slightly frozen for perfectly thin, tender pieces that cook in minutes.

Tip: The technique used in this recipe is called ***velveting***. This technique is commonly used in Chinese cooking to both lock in flavor and give the meat a soft, tender texture.

Per Serving: Calories: 287; Protein: 24g; Total carbs: 11g; Fiber: 2g; Fat: 16g

Apple-Cinnamon Slow Cooker Pork Loin

SERVINGS: 6 / PREP TIME: 10 MINUTES / COOK TIME: 6 HOURS

This cozy, slow-cooked dish brings sweet and savory together. Lean pork loin pairs beautifully with apples and cinnamon, a combo that feels indulgent but fits perfectly into your goals. Plus, cinnamon adds bold flavor without the need for extra salt. Set it, forget it, and come home to a comforting, protein-rich meal.

1 (2-pound) pork tenderloin
½ teaspoon salt
½ teaspoon freshly ground black pepper
3 teaspoons ground cinnamon, divided
1 tablespoon organic canola oil
2 onions, each cut into 6 wedges
3 firm, sweet apples (such as Honeycrisp or Fuji), cored and cut into wedges
¼ cup water

1. Cut 8 to 10 slits about 1 inch deep on one side of the pork tenderloin. Sprinkle the sides of the tenderloin with the salt, pepper, and 1 teaspoon of cinnamon.
2. In a large skillet, heat the oil over medium-high heat. Brown the tenderloin on all sides.
3. Cover the bottom of the slow cooker with the onion wedges and a few apple wedges. Sprinkle them with the remaining 2 teaspoons of cinnamon. Pour in the water.
4. Place the tenderloin on top of the onions and apples, and stuff the remaining apples into the slits of the pork.
5. Cover and cook on low for 6 hours. Slice the pork and serve with the onions and apples.

Tip: For easy cleanup when using a slow cooker, buy slow cooker inserts, which line the cooker before cooking. This way, when you are done, you can simply throw the insert away and the appliance can be wiped clean, ready for the next use.

Per Serving: Calories: 213; Protein: 19g; Total carbs: 16g; Fiber: 3g; Fat: 8g

Slow Cooker Pulled-Pork Sandwich

SERVINGS: 8 / PREP TIME: 10 MINUTES / COOK TIME: 4 TO 5 HOURS

This set-it-and-forget-it meal is as satisfying as it is simple. Lean, slow-cooked pork turns tender and flavorful with minimal effort, perfect for busy days when you want dinner ready the moment you walk in the door. Serve it on a whole grain bun or in a lettuce wrap for a high-protein take on a classic comfort food.

- 1 (2-pound) pork tenderloin
- ½ cup ketchup
- 3 tablespoons tomato paste
- 2 tablespoons apple cider vinegar
- 2 tablespoons Worcestershire sauce
- 1 tablespoon maple syrup
- 1 tablespoon brown mustard
- 8 whole wheat sandwich rolls

1. Place the pork in the slow cooker.
2. In a small bowl, whisk together the ketchup, tomato paste, vinegar, Worcestershire, maple syrup, and mustard. Pour the mixture over the pork.
3. Cover and cook the pork on low for 4 to 5 hours.
4. Using two forks, shred the meat and mix it back into the sauce.
5. Serve the pulled pork on the sandwich rolls.

Per Serving: Calories: 316; Protein: 25g; Total carbs: 34g; Fiber: 4g; Fat: 8g

Spaghetti Squash Lasagna Bowls

SERVINGS: 4 / PREP TIME: 10 MINUTES / COOK TIME: 1 HOUR

This lighter twist on lasagna swaps noodles for fiber-rich spaghetti squash so you get the comfort of a classic without the carb crash. Packed with protein, veggies, and melty cheese, these bowls are hearty and flavorful. Plus, using the squash halves as built-in bowls makes this a fun, no-fuss, all-in-one meal.

- 2 small spaghetti squash
- 8 ounces extra-lean ground beef
- 1 small onion, diced
- 1 (15-ounce) can diced tomatoes, drained
- 1 teaspoon Italian seasoning
- ½ teaspoon salt
- ½ teaspoon freshly ground black pepper
- ½ cup reduced-fat ricotta cheese
- ½ cup shredded mozzarella cheese

Tip: In anticipation of a busy night, prepare the entire recipe through step 6 the day before, then refrigerate, covered, until ready to cook. Bake the squash at 350°F until heated through and the cheese is browned, about 30 minutes.

1. Preheat the oven to 350°F.
2. Carefully cut each spaghetti squash in half lengthwise and remove any seeds with a spoon. Place the squash halves cut-side down in a large baking pan and pour in about ½ inch of water. Cook until the squash can easily be pierced, 30 to 45 minutes.
3. Remove the squash from the oven, let it cool for 10 minutes, and use a fork to remove and reserve the flesh, leaving about ¼ inch of flesh attached to each shell. Arrange the shells cut-side up on the baking dish.
4. In a skillet, brown the ground beef over medium-high heat. Add the diced onion and continue cooking, stirring regularly, until it becomes translucent. Add the tomatoes, Italian seasoning, salt, and pepper and stir to combine. Continue cooking until heated through.
5. Fold in the reserved squash flesh and remove the pan from the heat. Fold the ricotta cheese into the mixture.
6. Pack each squash shell with ¼ of the meat and squash mixture, packing it firmly as you go. Add 2 tablespoons of mozzarella cheese to the top of each squash.
7. Return the baking dish to the oven and bake until the cheese is melted and browned on top, 5 to 6 minutes.

Per Serving: Calories: 255; Protein: 20g; Total carbs: 14g; Fiber: 4g; Fat: 13g

Thai-Style Chicken Roll-Ups

SERVINGS: 2 / PREP TIME: 15 MINUTES

These fresh, flavorful roll-ups are one of our favorite lunch go-tos. They are quick to assemble, packed with protein, and bursting with Thai-inspired flavor. Prepping the components ahead of time means you can roll one up in under 5 minutes, making it easy to stay on track even during your busiest weeks. Real food, real fast, and seriously satisfying.

- 1 cup shredded cooked chicken breast
- 1 cup bean sprouts
- 1 cup shredded green cabbage
- ½ cup shredded carrots
- ¼ cup chopped scallions, both white and green parts
- ¼ cup chopped fresh cilantro
- 2 tablespoons natural peanut butter
- 2 tablespoons water
- 1 tablespoon rice wine vinegar
- 1 garlic clove, minced
- ¼ teaspoon salt
- 4 (8-inch) low-carb whole wheat tortillas

1. In a large mixing bowl, toss the chicken breast, bean sprouts, cabbage, carrots, scallions, and cilantro.
2. In a medium bowl, whisk together the peanut butter, water, vinegar, garlic, and salt.
3. Fill each tortilla with about 1 cup of the chicken and vegetable mixture. Spoon a tablespoon of sauce over the filling.
4. Fold in two opposite sides of the tortilla and roll up. Serve.

Substitution tip: For a lighter meal, use large lettuce leaves in place of the tortillas, or simply serve the dish as a salad.

Per Serving: Calories: 369; Protein: 36g; Total carbs: 36g; Fiber: 16g; Fat: 16g

Beef and Mushroom Burgers with Brie

SERVINGS: 6 / PREP TIME: 15 MINUTES / COOK TIME: 20 MINUTES

This juicy, flavor-packed burger uses cremini mushrooms to stretch the beef and cut fat without sacrificing satisfaction. The result? A hearty, high-protein meal that feels indulgent but supports your goals. Brie adds a creamy finish, and using extra-lean beef keeps the burgers lower in fat. Perfect for burger night with a smarter twist.

12 ounces cremini mushrooms
2 teaspoons canola or vegetable oil
½ teaspoon salt
½ teaspoon freshly ground black pepper
1 pound extra-lean ground beef
½ cup chopped onion
1 large egg, beaten
6 whole wheat hamburger buns
6 slices Brie cheese

1. In a food processor, pulse the mushrooms until they are coarsely ground.
2. In a large skillet, heat the oil over medium-high heat. Add the mushrooms, salt, and pepper and cook, stirring frequently, until the mushrooms brown and the juices evaporate. Remove from the heat and allow to cool for 10 minutes.
3. In a mixing bowl, combine the mushrooms, beef, onion, and egg. Form the mixture into 6 patties, pressing firmly so they hold together.
4. Reheat the large skillet over medium-high heat. Add the burgers and cook for 4 to 5 minutes per side. Place the burgers on the buns, top with cheese, and serve.

Per Serving: Calories: 412; Protein: 30g; Total carbs: 30g; 26g; Fiber: 4g; Fat: 18g

Turkey Chili

SERVINGS: 6 / PREP TIME: 15 MINUTES / COOK TIME: 30 MINUTES

This hearty, high-protein chili is comfort food that works for your goals, not against them. Made with lean turkey, fiber-rich beans, and bold spices, it keeps you full and satisfied. It's lower in sodium than most store-bought versions but still loaded with flavor. A go-to meal prep win for fat loss, maintenance, or just a cozy night in.

- 1 tablespoon extra virgin olive oil
- 1½ pounds lean ground turkey
- 1 large onion, diced
- 3 garlic cloves, minced
- 1 red bell pepper, seeded and diced
- 1 cup chopped celery
- 2 tablespoons chili powder
- 1 tablespoon ground cumin
- 1 (28-ounce) can reduced-salt diced tomatoes
- 1 (15-ounce) can reduced-sodium kidney beans, drained and rinsed
- 2 cups reduced-sodium chicken broth
- ½ teaspoon salt
- Shredded Cheddar cheese, for serving (optional)

1. In a large pot, heat the oil over medium heat. Add the turkey, onion, and garlic, and cook, stirring regularly, until the turkey is cooked through.
2. Add the bell pepper, celery, chili powder, and cumin. Stir well and continue to cook for 1 minute.
3. Add the tomatoes with their liquid, kidney beans, and chicken broth. Bring to a boil, reduce the heat to low, and simmer for 20 minutes.
4. Season with the salt and serve topped with cheese (if using).

Option tip: If you like a little heat in your chili, add 1 seeded and diced serrano or jalapeño pepper in step 2 along with the bell pepper, celery, and spices.

Per Serving: Calories: 275; Protein: 23g; Total carbs: 18g; Fiber: 5g; Fat: 14g

Easy Chicken Cacciatore

SERVINGS: 4 / PREP TIME: 10 MINUTES / COOK TIME: 45 MINUTES

This Italian-inspired classic is naturally low in carbs, high in protein, and full of real-food flavor, making it a perfect fit for your fat-loss or maintenance plan. With tender chicken, herbs, and plenty of veggies, it's a satisfying dish you can feel good about. Make it once and enjoy the leftovers the next day, because easy, delicious meals should work for you.

- 3 teaspoons extra virgin olive oil, divided
- 1 pound chicken thighs (substitute chicken breast for a lower-fat option)
- 8 ounces brown mushrooms
- 1 large onion, sliced
- 1 red bell pepper, seeded and cut into strips
- 3 garlic cloves, minced
- ½ cup dry red wine
- 1 (28-ounce) can whole tomatoes, drained
- 1 thyme sprig
- 1 rosemary sprig
- ½ teaspoon salt
- ¼ teaspoon freshly ground black pepper
- ¼ cup water

1. Preheat the oven to 350°F.
2. In a Dutch oven, heat 2 teaspoons of oil over medium-high heat. Place the chicken in the Dutch oven and sear it on all sides until browned. Remove and set aside.
3. Heat the remaining 1 teaspoon of oil in the Dutch oven and sauté the mushrooms for 3 to 5 minutes, until they brown and begin to release their water.
4. Add the onion, bell pepper, and garlic, and mix together with the mushrooms. Cook an additional 3 to 5 minutes until the onion begins to soften.
5. Add the red wine and deglaze the pot, stirring to scrape up the brown bits from the bottom. Bring to a simmer. Add the tomatoes, breaking them into pieces with a spoon. Add the thyme, rosemary, salt, and pepper to the pot and mix well.
6. Add the water, then nestle the seared chicken, along with any juices that have accumulated, in the vegetables.
7. Transfer the pot to the oven. Cook for 30 minutes until the chicken is cooked through and its juices run clear.
8. Remove the thyme and rosemary sprigs and serve.

Meal tip: Complete this Italian plate by pairing with Crispy Parmesan Cups with White Beans and Veggies (page 125).

Per Serving: Calories: 377; Protein: 23g; Total carbs: 16g; Fiber: 4g; Fat: 22g

Quick Weeknight Chicken Parmesan

SERVINGS: 4 / PREP TIME: 10 MINUTES / COOK TIME: 30 MINUTES

This high-protein, comfort-food classic is a great example of "cook once, eat twice": Make extra and repurpose it for tomorrow's lunch or dinner. This pairs well with veggies, pasta, or garlic bread.

½ cup rolled oats
¼ teaspoon freshly ground black pepper
1 large egg
2 tablespoons unsweetened plain almond milk
¼ cup grated parmesan cheese
¼ cup whole wheat breadcrumbs
4 boneless, skinless chicken breast cutlets (about 1 pound total)
1 cup marinara sauce
¼ cup shredded mozzarella cheese

1. Preheat the oven to 400°F.
2. In a blender or food processor, process the oats until they resemble flour. Transfer to a medium bowl and mix with the pepper.
3. In another medium bowl, combine the egg and almond milk and lightly beat.
4. On a plate, mix the parmesan cheese with the breadcrumbs.
5. One at a time, roll the chicken pieces in the oat flour, dip them in the egg mixture, and roll them in the parmesan-breadcrumb mixture. Arrange the chicken pieces in a single layer in a baking dish.
6. Bake for 25 minutes until the chicken is cooked through and the coating is browned.
7. Spoon half of the marinara over the chicken and sprinkle with cheese. Bake 5 more minutes.
8. Top with the remaining marinara sauce. Serve alongside cooked pasta, if desired.

Substitution tip: If you want something lighter, try using a large portobello mushroom instead of chicken. Lightly wet the mushroom before rolling it in the flour, and continue with the recipe as written for a vegetarian take on the original.

Per Serving: Calories: 275; Protein: 33g; Total carbs: 16g; Fiber: 2g; Fat: 9g

Mango-Glazed Pork Tenderloin Roast

SERVINGS: 4 / PREP TIME: 10 MINUTES / COOK TIME: 20 MINUTES

This lean, flavorful roast is proof that healthy eating can be beautiful, satisfying, and full of bold flavor. Mango adds natural sweetness while fresh herbs bring balance and depth. It's a high-protein, metabolism-friendly main that fills your kitchen with incredible aromas and your plate with goodness. Pairs nicely with whole grains like quinoa or brown rice.

1½-pound boneless pork tenderloin, trimmed of fat
1 teaspoon chopped fresh rosemary
1 teaspoon chopped fresh thyme
½ teaspoon salt, divided
½ teaspoon freshly ground black pepper, divided
1 teaspoon extra virgin olive oil
1 tablespoon honey
2 tablespoons white wine vinegar
2 tablespoons dry cooking wine
1 tablespoon minced fresh ginger
1 cup diced mango

1. Preheat the oven to 400°F.
2. Season the tenderloin with the rosemary, the thyme, and half the salt and pepper.
3. Heat the olive oil in an oven-safe skillet over medium-high heat, and sear the tenderloin until browned on all sides, about 5 minutes total.
4. Transfer the skillet to the oven and roast for 12 to 15 minutes, until the pork is cooked through, the juices run clear, and the internal temperature reaches 145°F. Transfer the pork to a cutting board to rest for 5 minutes. Set the skillet back on the stovetop.
5. In a small bowl, combine the honey, vinegar, cooking wine, and ginger.
6. Into the same skillet, pour the honey mixture and simmer for 1 minute. Add the mango and toss to coat.
7. Transfer the mixture to a blender and puree until smooth. Season with the remaining salt and pepper.
8. Slice the pork into rounds and serve with the mango sauce.

Per Serving: Calories: 265; Protein: 34g; Total carbs: 11g; Fiber: 1g; Fat: 8g

CHAPTER 8

Veggie Mains

Falafel with Creamy Garlic-Yogurt Sauce

SERVINGS: 4 / PREP TIME: 15 MINUTES / COOK TIME: 10 MINUTES

Falafel doesn't have to be takeout only. This easy homemade version uses chickpeas for a fiber-rich, satisfying meal. Paired with a creamy garlic-yogurt sauce, it's a flavorful, balanced dish that fits perfectly into your fat-loss or maintenance plan without sacrificing taste or convenience.

FOR THE SAUCE

1 cup plain nonfat Greek yogurt
3 garlic cloves, minced
Juice of 1 lemon
1 tablespoon extra virgin olive oil
¼ teaspoon salt

FOR THE FALAFEL

1 (15-ounce) can reduced-sodium chickpeas, drained and rinsed
¾ cup cooked quinoa
½ cup cooked hemp seeds
2 garlic cloves, roughly chopped
2 tablespoons whole wheat flour
2 tablespoons chopped fresh parsley
½ teaspoon ground cumin
¼ teaspoon salt
2 teaspoons canola oil, divided
8 large lettuce leaves, chopped
1 cucumber, chopped
1 tomato, diced

TO MAKE THE SAUCE

In a small bowl, combine the yogurt, garlic, lemon juice, olive oil, and salt, and mix well. Cover and refrigerate until ready to serve.

TO MAKE THE FALAFEL

1. In a food processor or blender, combine the chickpeas, quinoa, hemps seeds, and garlic, and pulse until chopped well but not creamy.
2. Add the flour, parsley, cumin, and salt. Pulse several more times until incorporated.
3. Using your hands, form the mixture into 8 balls, using about 1 tablespoon of the mixture for each ball.
4. In a medium skillet, heat 1 teaspoon of canola oil over medium-high heat. Working in batches, add the falafel to the skillet, cooking on each side for 2 to 3 minutes until browned and crisp.
5. Remove the falafel from the skillet, and repeat with the remaining oil and falafel until all are cooked.
6. Divide the lettuce, cucumber, and tomato among four plates. Top each plate with two falafel balls and four tablespoons of sauce. Serve immediately.

Per Serving: Calories: 273; Protein: 15g; Total carbs: 27g; Fiber: 6g; Fat: 13g

Mozzarella and Artichoke–Stuffed Spaghetti Squash

SERVINGS: 2 / PREP TIME: 10 MINUTES / COOK TIME: 45 MINUTES

This delicious squash bowl is a family favorite and a fantastic way to enjoy a lower-carb, nutrient-packed pasta substitute. The spaghetti squash's unique texture pairs perfectly with creamy mozzarella and tender artichokes for a comforting, flavorful meal that supports your goals. Plus, it's fun to make and even more fun to eat—*bon appétit*!

1 small spaghetti squash, halved and seeded
1 cup low-fat cottage cheese
¼ cup shredded mozzarella cheese, divided
2 garlic cloves, minced
1 cup chopped artichoke hearts
1 cup thinly sliced kale
½ teaspoon salt
Pinch freshly ground black pepper

1. Preheat the oven to 400°F. Line a baking sheet with parchment paper.
2. Place the cut squash halves on the prepared baking sheet cut-side down and roast for 30 to 40 minutes, depending on the size and thickness of the squash, until they are fork-tender. Set aside to cool slightly.
3. In a large bowl, mix the cottage cheese, 2 tablespoons of mozzarella cheese, garlic, artichoke hearts, kale, salt, and pepper.
4. Preheat the broiler to high.
5. Using a fork, break apart the flesh of the spaghetti squash into strands, being careful to leave the skin intact. Add the strands to the cheese and vegetable mixture. Toss gently to combine.
6. Divide the mixture between the two hollowed-out squash halves and top with the remaining 2 tablespoons of cheese.

Per Serving: Calories: 358; Protein: 29g; Total carbs: 51g; Fiber: 12g; Fat: 8g

Sweet Potato, Tofu, Chickpea, and Kale Bowl with Creamy Tahini Sauce

SERVINGS: 2 / PREP TIME: 10 MINUTES / COOK TIME: 15 MINUTES

This warm, nourishing bowl is perfect for cozy winter meals; it's packed with plant-based protein, fiber, and vibrant veggies. The creamy tahini sauce adds rich, savory flavor and healthy fats that keep you satisfied. If you haven't tried tahini yet, this recipe is a delicious introduction; you might find yourself using it on everything. For a tasty twist, swap black beans for chickpeas.

FOR THE SAUCE

½ cup plain nonfat Greek yogurt
2 tablespoons tahini
2 tablespoons hemp seeds
1 garlic clove, minced
Pinch salt
Freshly ground black pepper

FOR THE BOWL

1 small sweet potato, peeled and finely diced
2 teaspoons extra virgin olive oil, divided
6 ounces tofu
½ cup from 1 (15-ounce) can reduced-sodium chickpeas, drained and rinsed
2 cups baby kale

TO MAKE THE SAUCE

1. In a small bowl, whisk together the yogurt and tahini.
2. Stir in the hemp seeds, garlic, and salt. Season with pepper.
3. Add 2 to 3 tablespoons water to create a creamy yet pourable consistency. Set aside.

TO MAKE THE BOWL

1. Preheat the oven to 425°F. Line a baking sheet with parchment paper.
2. Arrange the sweet potato on the prepared baking sheet and drizzle with 1 teaspoon of the olive oil. Toss. Roast for 10 to 15 minutes, stirring once, until tender and browned.
3. While the potatoes cook, cut the tofu into 1-inch cubes. Heat a skillet over medium-high heat and add the remaining 1 teaspoon of the oil. Cook until lightly browned.
4. In each of 2 bowls, arrange half of the chickpeas, 1 cup of kale, and half of the cooked sweet potato. Drizzle with creamy tahini sauce and serve.

Per Serving: Calories: 390; Protein: 22g; Total carbs: 28g; Fiber: 7g; Fat: 21g

Black Bean Enchilada Skillet Casserole

SERVINGS: 6 / PREP TIME: 15 MINUTES / COOK TIME: 15 MINUTES

This one-dish skillet casserole is a weeknight hero. It's bursting with bold flavors and plant-based protein, making it a filling meal you can have on the table in under 30 minutes.

1 tablespoon extra virgin olive oil
½ onion, chopped
½ red bell pepper, seeded and chopped
½ green bell pepper, seeded and chopped
2 small zucchini, chopped
3 garlic cloves, minced
1 (15-ounce) can reduced-sodium black beans, drained and rinsed
1 (15-ounce) can cannellini beans
1 (16-ounce) package tofu
1 cup fat-free Greek yogurt, plus more for serving
1 (10-ounce) can reduced-sodium enchilada sauce
1 teaspoon ground cumin
¼ teaspoon salt
¼ teaspoon freshly ground black pepper
½ cup shredded Cheddar cheese, divided
2 (6-inch) corn tortillas, cut into strips
Chopped fresh cilantro, for garnish

1. Preheat the broiler to high.
2. In a large oven-safe skillet, heat the oil over medium-high heat.
3. Add the onion, red bell pepper, green bell pepper, zucchini, and garlic to the skillet, and cook for 3 to 5 minutes, until the onion softens.
4. Add the black beans, cannellini beans, tofu, Greek yogurt, enchilada sauce, cumin, salt, pepper, ¼ cup of cheese, and tortilla strips, and mix together. Top with the remaining ¼ cup of cheese.
5. Put the skillet under the broiler and broil for 5 to 8 minutes, until the cheese is melted and bubbly.
6. Garnish with cilantro and serve with yogurt on the side.

Per Serving: Calories: 245; Protein: 17g; Total carbs: 24g; Fiber: 7g; Fat: 8g

Cheesy Garlic Pasta Salad

SERVINGS: 4 / PREP TIME: 5 TO 10 MINUTES / COOK TIME: 5 MINUTES

Think pasta is off limits? Think again. This comforting, veggie-packed pasta salad proves you can enjoy your favorites. It's full of flavor, fiber, and balanced ingredients that keep you satisfied and on track. Bonus: It tastes even better after a day or two, making it perfect for meal prep or potlucks.

- 6 asparagus spears, trimmed and cut into 1-inch pieces
- 1 teaspoon extra virgin olive oil
- Freshly ground black pepper
- 3 cups cooked chickpea penne pasta
- 3 ounces goat cheese
- ¾ cup cherry tomatoes, quartered
- ½ cup diced yellow bell pepper
- 2 garlic cloves, minced
- 1 cup chopped arugula
- 3 large basil leaves, minced
- Pinch salt

1. Preheat the broiler to high. Line a baking sheet with aluminum foil.
2. Put the asparagus on the lined baking sheet. Drizzle with the olive oil and season with black pepper. Broil for 5 minutes.
3. If the pasta is not already warm, heat it in the microwave for about 30 seconds. Put the pasta in a large mixing bowl. Add the goat cheese, tomatoes, bell pepper, garlic, arugula, and basil. Stir to combine well.
4. Add the asparagus to the pasta mixture. Season with a pinch each of salt and freshly ground pepper.

Per Serving: Calories: 310; Protein: 15g; Total carbs: 33g; Fiber: 6g; Fat: 12g

Crisp Vegetable and Quinoa Bowl

SERVINGS: 4 / PREP TIME: 15 MINUTES / COOK TIME: 15 MINUTES

This vibrant bowl combines protein-packed quinoa with a crunchy medley of green veggies such as asparagus, peas, cucumber, and spinach for a meal that's light yet filling. Topped with a creamy, garlicky dressing, it delivers satisfying texture and flavor while supporting your metabolism and keeping cravings at bay. Perfect for a nourishing lunch or dinner.

¾ cup plain 2% Greek yogurt
¼ cup freshly squeezed lemon juice
2 tablespoons extra virgin olive oil
6 garlic cloves, minced
½ teaspoon salt
1 cup quinoa
2 cups water
1 pound asparagus, cut into 2-inch pieces
1 cup fresh or frozen green peas
1 cup frozen shelled edamame
1 cucumber, peeled, halved lengthwise, and thinly sliced crosswise
8 cups baby spinach
½ cup walnut pieces

1. In a small bowl, whisk together the yogurt, lemon juice, olive oil, garlic, and salt. Set aside.
2. In a small pot, combine the quinoa and water. Bring to a boil over medium-high heat. Reduce the heat, cover, and simmer until tender, about 10 minutes. Drain any remaining water and spread out the quinoa on a baking sheet to cool.
3. Bring a large pot of water to a boil over medium-high heat. Add the asparagus, peas, and edamame, and cook until they are crisp-tender, about 2 minutes. Drain and run the vegetables under cold water to stop them from cooking.
4. Divide the quinoa among four bowls. Top each bowl with equal amounts of asparagus, peas, edamame, cucumber, spinach, and walnuts. Drizzle the dressing over the bowls and serve.

Tip: For easy prep of salads like this, cook double the amount of quinoa needed and store the extra in an airtight container in the refrigerator for up to 5 days. When needed, simply cut the veggies, make the dressing, and toss with the quinoa for a healthy version of fast food.

Per Serving: Calories: 460; Protein: 20g; Total carbs: 39g; Fiber: 7g; Fat: 26g

Broccoli-Almond-Sesame Soba Noodles with Tempeh

SERVINGS: 4 / PREP TIME: 10 MINUTES, PLUS 1 HOUR TO CHILL / COOK TIME: 30 MINUTES

This comforting noodle bowl is lower in carbs and blood-sugar friendly, tossed with a savory sesame dressing. Make sure to check the label and only buy "100% buckwheat soba."

12 ounces tempeh
2 tablespoons extra virgin olive oil
Salt
¼ cup sliced almonds
6 ounces dried buckwheat soba noodles
1 cup fresh or frozen broccoli florets
2 tablespoons reduced-sodium soy sauce
1 tablespoon rice vinegar
2 teaspoons honey
2 teaspoons toasted sesame oil
½ cup sliced sugar snap or snow peas
1 bunch scallions (green and white parts), finely chopped
1 red bell pepper, seeded and sliced

1. Preheat the oven to 400°F.
2. Cut the tempeh into 1-inch pieces. In a baking dish, toss the tempeh with olive oil and a pinch of salt. Bake for 20 minutes and set aside.
3. Heat a small skillet over medium-high heat. Toast the almonds, shaking the pan continuously, until just browned, 2 to 3 minutes. Remove the almonds from the pan and set aside.
4. Bring a large pot of water to a boil over high heat. Add the noodles. Cook according to the package directions. Drain the noodles and run them under cold water until cool to the touch. Put the noodles in a large bowl.
5. Meanwhile, fill another large pot with a couple inches of water and a steamer basket. Bring the water to a boil over high heat and add the broccoli. Cover and steam the broccoli until fork-tender yet still bright green, 3 to 5 minutes.
6. Remove the broccoli from the basket and run it under cold water until cool. Transfer it to the bowl with the noodles.
7. In a small bowl, whisk together the soy sauce, vinegar, honey, and sesame oil.
8. Add the tempeh, peas, scallions, bell pepper, toasted almonds, and soy sauce mixture to the noodles and broccoli. Toss well to combine. Refrigerate for at least 1 hour before serving to allow the flavors to meld.

Per Serving: Calories: 460; Protein: 22g; Total carbs: 37g; Fiber: 7g; Fat: 26g

Pasta with Sun-Dried Tomatoes, Feta Cheese, and Arugula

SERVINGS: 4 / PREP TIME: 5 MINUTES / COOK TIME: 15 MINUTES

This quick, comforting pasta dish is perfect for busy weeknights when you want something satisfying fast. Simple ingredients come together to create earthy, bold flavors with peppery arugula, tangy sun-dried tomatoes, and creamy feta, all balanced for a meal that's both delicious and nourishing. A smart choice when time is short but flavor is nonnegotiable.

½ pound high-protein penne pasta
2 tablespoons extra virgin olive oil
3 garlic cloves, minced
½ cup sun-dried tomatoes
½ cup reduced-fat feta cheese, crumbled
¼ teaspoon salt
¼ teaspoon freshly ground black pepper
3 cups arugula

1. Bring a large pot of water to a boil over high heat. Cook the pasta according to the package directions. Drain.
2. In a large skillet, heat the olive oil over medium-high heat. Add the garlic and sauté until just fragrant. Add the sun-dried tomatoes and cook for 1 additional minute, stirring constantly.
3. Add the cooked noodles to the skillet and sprinkle with the feta cheese, salt, and pepper. Stir to combine.
4. Add the arugula, toss, and serve.

Per Serving: Calories: 375; Protein: 17g; Total carbs: 39g; Fiber: 4g; Fat: 16g

Sprouted Grain and Curried Cauliflower Bowls

SERVINGS: 4 / PREP TIME: 10 MINUTES / COOK TIME: 30 MINUTES

Rye and other sprouted grains bring a unique, nutty flavor and plenty of fiber to this warming, spiced cauliflower bowl. If you haven't cooked with rye before, this recipe is a delicious introduction and a great way to enjoy nutrient-rich grains that support lasting fullness.

- 1 large head cauliflower, divided into florets
- 1 tablespoon extra virgin olive oil, plus ¼ cup
- 1 teaspoon sea salt
- 1 teaspoon curry powder
- ½ teaspoon smoked paprika
- 4 cups sprouted rye berries or sprouted grain of choice
- 1 (15-ounce) can chickpeas, drained and rinsed
- ½ cup pumpkin seeds
- ¼ cup sliced scallions, green and white parts
- 2 teaspoons protein powder (pea works best)
- Grated zest and juice of 1 large lemon
- ½ teaspoon freshly ground black pepper

1. Preheat the oven to 400°F. Line a baking sheet with parchment paper.
2. In a bowl, toss together the cauliflower, 1 tablespoon of oil, the salt, the curry powder, and the paprika.
3. Spread the cauliflower out in a single layer on the prepared baking sheet.
4. Transfer the baking sheet to the oven and roast for about 30 minutes, until the cauliflower is tender and golden. Remove from the oven.
5. In a large skillet, warm the rye berries and chickpeas slightly, or microwave for about 1 minute. Remove from the heat.
6. In a large bowl, toss together the rye berries, chickpeas, cauliflower, pumpkin seeds, scallions, protein powder, remaining ¼ cup of olive oil, lemon zest, lemon juice, and pepper. Adjust the seasoning with more salt and pepper as needed.

Per Serving: Calories: 480; Protein: 18g; Total carbs: 45g; Fiber: 8g; Fat: 26g

Crispy Parmesan Cups with White Beans and Veggies

SERVINGS: 2 / PREP TIME: 15 MINUTES / COOK TIME: 10 MINUTES

Simple, quick meals are key to staying on track, and these crispy cups deliver flavor and nourishment in just minutes. Packed with fiber-rich white beans and vibrant veggies, they're a satisfying way to curb hunger and enjoy real food without the stress of complicated cooking.

- 1 cup grated parmesan cheese, divided (confirm vegetarian-friendly, if needed)
- 1 (15-ounce) can reduced-sodium cannellini beans, drained and rinsed
- 1 cucumber, peeled and finely diced
- ½ cup finely diced red onion
- ¼ cup thinly sliced fresh basil
- 1 garlic clove, minced
- ½ jalapeño pepper, diced
- 1 tablespoon extra virgin olive oil
- 1 tablespoon balsamic vinegar
- ¼ teaspoon salt
- Freshly ground black pepper

1. Heat a medium nonstick skillet over medium heat. Sprinkle 2 tablespoons of cheese in a thin circle in the center of the pan, flattening it with a spatula.
2. When the cheese melts, use a spatula to flip the cheese and lightly brown the other side.
3. Remove the cheese "pancake" from the pan and place it into the cup of a muffin tin, bending it gently with your hands to fit in the muffin cup.
4. Repeat with the remaining cheese until you have 8 cups.
5. In a mixing bowl, combine the beans, cucumber, onion, basil, garlic, jalapeño, olive oil, and vinegar, and season with the salt and pepper.
6. When cheese cups are cool and firm, fill each cup with the bean mixture, remove them from the pan, and serve.

Per Serving: Calories: 494; Protein: 29g; Total carbs: 48g; Fiber: 15g; Fat: 21g

CHAPTER 9

Sides

Roasted Lemon and Garlic Broccoli

SERVINGS: 8 / PREP TIME: 10 MINUTES / COOK TIME: 25 MINUTES

This easy, flavor-packed side is a go-to for adding fiber, volume, and nutrients to your plate. Roasting brings out broccoli's natural sweetness, while garlic and lemon juice keep it bright and crave-worthy. This side pairs effortlessly with fish, chicken, or plant-based mains, and it helps fill you up with fiber that supports digestion and blood-sugar balance.

2 large broccoli heads, cut into florets
3 garlic cloves, minced
2 tablespoons extra virgin olive oil
¼ teaspoon salt
¼ teaspoon freshly ground black pepper
2 tablespoons freshly squeezed lemon juice

1. Preheat the oven to 425°F.
2. On a rimmed baking sheet, toss the broccoli, garlic, and olive oil. Season with the salt and pepper.
3. Roast, tossing occasionally, for 25 to 30 minutes until tender and browned.
4. Season with the lemon juice and serve.

Substitution tip: This recipe also works well with Brussels sprouts, cauliflower, and even broccoli rabe.

Per Serving: Calories: 61; Protein: 2g; Total carbs: 6g; Fiber: 2g; Fat: 4g

Spicy Roasted Cauliflower with Lime

SERVINGS: 4 / PREP TIME: 5 MINUTES / COOK TIME: 10 MINUTES

Cauliflower has earned its spot as a go-to side for good reason: It's low in carbs, high in fiber, and takes on bold flavors like a champ. Roasting brings out its natural sweetness, while a kick of spice and a squeeze of lime make it totally crave-worthy. It's a smart way to bulk up your plate and stay full, all without starch.

1 cauliflower head, broken into small florets
2 tablespoons extra virgin olive oil
½ teaspoon ground chipotle chili powder
½ teaspoon salt
Juice of I lime

1. Preheat the oven to 450°F. Line a rimmed baking sheet with parchment paper.
2. In a large mixing bowl, toss the cauliflower with the olive oil, chipotle chili powder, and salt. Arrange in a single layer on the prepared baking sheet.
3. Roast for 15 minutes, flip, and continue to roast for 15 more minutes, until well-browned and tender.
4. Sprinkle with the lime juice, adjust the salt as needed, and serve.

Ingredient tip: Chipotle chili powder is a mild chili powder that lends a smoky flavor to foods. Find it at specialty spice shops and well-stocked grocery stores.

Per Serving: Calories: 100; Protein: 3g; Total carbs: 8g; Fiber: 3g; Fat: 7g

Sautéed Garlic, Ginger, and Shallot Green Beans

SERVINGS: 4 / PREP TIME: 10 MINUTES / COOK TIME: 10 MINUTES

These vibrant green beans are anything but boring. They're blanched for perfect texture, then sautéed with garlic, ginger, and shallots for a flavorful, nutrient-packed side. They're quick, easy, and pair perfectly with lean protein or plant-based mains. It's a simple way to add fiber and volume to any meal without overcomplicating your routine.

1 pound green beans, trimmed
1 tablespoon extra virgin olive oil
1 shallot, minced
2 garlic cloves, minced
2-inch knob ginger, minced
¼ teaspoon salt, plus more for the water

1. Fill a large bowl with ice water and set aside.
2. Bring a large pot of salted water to a boil over high heat. Add the beans and return the water to a boil. Cook until just tender but still bright green, about 3 minutes.
3. Use a slotted spoon to transfer the beans to the ice bath. Allow the beans to cool for 3 minutes, then transfer them to a colander to drain. Pat them dry with paper towels or a clean kitchen towel.
4. In a large skillet, heat the oil over medium heat. Add the shallot, garlic, and ginger, and sauté until the garlic turns a light golden brown and the shallot becomes tender.
5. Add the green beans to the skillet and toss until heated through, 2 to 3 minutes. Season with the salt and serve.

Per Serving: Calories: 82; Protein: 3g; Total carbs: 12g; Fiber: 4g; Fat: 3g

Five-Minute Brussels Sprouts and Almonds

SERVINGS: 4 / PREP TIME: 10 MINUTES / COOK TIME: 10 MINUTES

Short on time but still want something nutrient-dense and satisfying? This quick sautéed side delivers big on flavor and fiber, with crunchy almonds for healthy fats and texture. It's a perfect low-carb addition to any meal that's ready in minutes and ideal for days when you're busy but still want to eat with intention.

2 cups Brussels sprouts
¼ cup almonds
1 tablespoon extra virgin olive oil
2 garlic cloves, minced
¼ teaspoon freshly ground black pepper
¼ cup chopped fresh parsley
1 tablespoon grated parmesan cheese
Juice of ½ lime

1. Combine the Brussels sprouts and almonds in a food processor. Pulse a few times until very coarsely chopped.
2. In a large skillet, heat the olive oil over medium-high heat. Add the Brussels sprouts and almonds, and cook until the sprouts are slightly browned, 5 to 7 minutes.
3. Stir in the garlic and black pepper, and cook for an additional 2 to 3 minutes.
4. Turn off the heat and stir in the parsley. Sprinkle the parmesan cheese and lime juice over the top. Serve immediately.

Tip: Both almonds and Brussels sprouts are good sources of potassium, so eating this dish is an excellent way to include this important mineral in your diet. Since potassium helps regulate the fluids in our bodies while maintaining normal blood pressure, it's especially helpful for individuals with diabetes, who are at a higher risk of hypertension, also known as high blood pressure.

Per Serving: Calories: 111; Protein: 4g; Total carbs: 7g; Fiber: 3g; Fat: 8g

Mexi-Cauli Rice

SERVINGS: 4 / PREP TIME: 15 MINUTES / COOK TIME: 10 MINUTES

This flavorful, crowd-pleasing side is a smart swap for traditional rice. It's lower in carbs and higher in fiber. It pairs perfectly with lean protein, works great as a base for bowls or tacos, and even stands alone as a savory snack. A must-have for parties, meal prep, or weeknight dinners.

- 3 cups cauliflower florets
- 1 tablespoon extra virgin olive oil
- ½ cup diced onions
- 2 or 3 sliced tomatoes
- 1 teaspoon garlic powder
- Pinch cayenne pepper
- ¼ cup chopped fresh cilantro
- Juice of ½ lime
- ½ teaspoon salt
- ½ teaspoon freshly ground black pepper

1. In a food processor, pulse the cauliflower a few times until it is in small, rice-like pieces.
2. In a large skillet, heat the olive oil over medium-high heat. Add the cauliflower and onions, and sauté until the onions are translucent, 3 to 4 minutes.
3. Add the tomatoes and cook until they are broken down, 1 to 2 minutes. Stir in the garlic powder and cayenne pepper, and remove from the heat.
4. Stir in the cilantro, lime juice, and salt and pepper. Serve warm.

Per Serving: Calories: 75; Protein: 3g; Total carbs: 10g; Fiber: 3g; Fat: 4g

Mediterranean Oven-Roasted Potatoes and Vegetables with Herbs

SERVINGS: 6 / PREP TIME: 10 MINUTES / COOK TIME: 25 MINUTES

This vibrant, herb-infused medley is a staple in any balanced meal plan. Roasting brings out the natural sweetness of the potatoes and vegetables, while fresh Mediterranean herbs add flavor and antioxidants without extra sodium. It's a warm, satisfying side that complements any protein and keeps your meals both delicious and nutrient-dense.

- 8 ounces fingerling potatoes, quartered
- 8 ounces miniature red bell peppers, halved lengthwise and seeded
- 8 ounces mushrooms, sliced
- 1 cup cauliflower florets
- 1 onion, sliced
- 2 tablespoons extra virgin olive oil
- ½ teaspoon salt
- ½ teaspoon freshly ground black pepper
- 1 tablespoon chopped fresh rosemary
- 1 tablespoon chopped fresh oregano
- 1 tablespoon chopped fresh parsley

1. Preheat the oven to 425°F.
2. In a large bowl, combine the potatoes, peppers, mushrooms, cauliflower, and onion.
3. Drizzle with the olive oil, salt, and pepper, and toss to combine.
4. Arrange the vegetables in a single layer on a baking sheet. Bake for 25 minutes, stirring once halfway through.
5. Remove from the oven and toss with the rosemary, oregano, and parsley. Serve.

Per Serving: Calories: 96; Protein: 3g; Total carbs: 13g; Fiber: 2g; Fat: 5g

Wild Rice Pilaf with Broccoli and Carrots

SERVINGS: 8 / PREP TIME: 10 MINUTES / COOK TIME: 1 HOUR 30 MINUTES

This hearty pilaf combines wild and brown rice with fiber-rich veggies for a side dish that's as filling as it is flavorful. Wild rice adds a nutty bite and slow-digesting carbs, while broccoli and carrots bring color and nutrients to the plate. It's a simple, savory way to round out any protein-forward meal.

- Nonstick cooking spray
- 4 cups reduced-sodium chicken broth
- ¾ cup wild rice
- ¾ cup long-grain brown rice
- ¼ cup extra virgin olive oil
- 1 large onion, chopped
- 2 carrots, peeled and chopped
- ½ teaspoon dried thyme
- 2 garlic cloves, minced
- 3 cups broccoli florets
- 1 teaspoon salt
- ½ teaspoon freshly ground black pepper

1. Preheat the oven to 350°F. Lightly coat a 2-quart casserole dish with nonstick cooking spray.
2. In a large pot, combine the broth, wild rice, and brown rice. Bring to a boil over high heat, then reduce the heat to medium. Cover and cook until the water is absorbed and the rice is tender, about 45 minutes. Let stand for 10 minutes, covered.
3. In a large skillet, heat the olive oil over medium-high heat. Add the onion, carrots, and thyme, and sauté until the onion becomes translucent, 5 to 7 minutes. Add the garlic and sauté for 1 additional minute. Remove the skillet from the heat.
4. Stir in the broccoli, rice, salt, and pepper. Transfer the mixture to the casserole dish, cover, and bake until the broccoli is tender, about 30 minutes.

Per Serving: Calories: 219; Protein: 6g; Total carbs: 33g; Fiber: 3g; Fat: 8g

Crispy Sage-Roasted Root Vegetables

SERVINGS: 4 / PREP TIME: 5 MINUTES / COOK TIME: 35 MINUTES

Looking to fall back in love with veggies? This roasted medley of four different root vegetables, seasoned with fragrant sage, brings out a delicious variety of flavors and textures that might surprise you. It's a nutrient-packed, satisfying side that makes eating your veggies something to look forward to.

1 medium sweet potato, peeled and diced
2 new potatoes, diced
2 beets, diced
3 carrots, peeled and cut into 1-inch pieces
1 tablespoon extra virgin olive oil
15 fresh sage leaves
1 teaspoon garlic powder

1. Preheat the oven to 400°F. Line a baking sheet with parchment paper.
2. Toss together the sweet potato, new potatoes, beets, carrots, oil, sage, and garlic on the lined baking sheet.
3. Roast, tossing once halfway through, until the sweet potatoes are slightly browned and the beets are soft inside, 25 to 35 minutes.
4. Remove the sage leaves prior to serving.

Per Serving: Calories: 122; Protein: 3g; Total carbs: 21g; Fiber: 5g; Fat: 4g

Rice and Spinach Mold

SERVINGS: 4 TO 6 / PREP TIME: 15 MINUTES / COOK TIME: 50 MINUTES

This simple yet elegant dish turns nutrient-rich spinach into a satisfying side. It's an easy way to add color and nutrients to your plate.

- 1 tablespoon butter
- 3 tablespoons extra virgin olive oil
- 1 medium white onion, diced
- 1¾ cups basmati or other long-grain white rice
- 1 (10-ounce) bag frozen chopped spinach, thawed, all liquid pressed out
- 1 teaspoon salt
- ¼ teaspoon freshly ground black pepper
- 3½ cups vegetable broth or water
- ½ cup chopped sun-dried tomatoes
- 1 tablespoon grated lemon zest
- ½ cup parmesan cheese
- 2 eggs, beaten

1. Preheat the oven to 350°F.
2. Butter a 1½-quart soufflé dish or a metal bowl and set aside.
3. In a medium saucepan, place the olive oil and onion and sauté over medium heat until the onions have slightly browned, about 5 to 10 minutes.
4. Add the rice, spinach, salt, pepper, and broth or water and bring to a boil. Reduce to a simmer and cook, covered, for 15 to 20 minutes, or until all the liquid is absorbed and the rice is tender.
5. Spoon the rice mixture into a large bowl and fluff with a wooden spoon. Let it cool for 15 minutes.
6. Add the sun-dried tomatoes, lemon zest, parmesan cheese, and eggs to the rice and mix well.
7. Spoon the mixture into the buttered mold and press firmly. Smooth the top.
8. Cover the mold with a piece of foil and place it into a larger baking pan. Add boiling water to the larger pan, to reach halfway up the side of the mold. Bake for 30 minutes.
9. Remove the mold from the water and discard the foil. Place a serving dish over the mold and invert it onto the dish. Carefully remove mold and slice into wedges to serve.

Per Serving: Calories: 384; Protein: 10g; Total carbs: 41g; Fiber: 3g; Fat: 19g

Tip: If you don't have a 1½-quart soufflé dish or metal bowl, you can make this in an 8-by-13-inch pan. The success of this dish relies on how well you pack the rice into the mold, so press firmly when filling the mold.

Mashed Cauliflower and Potatoes

SERVINGS: 6 / PREP TIME: 15 MINUTES / COOK TIME: 20 MINUTES

This lighter take on classic mashed potatoes blends creamy cauliflower with a touch of potato for a lower-carb, higher-fiber side. Keeping the skins on boosts nutrients and adds texture, making it a satisfying complement to any lean protein and non-starchy veggie. Comfort food that supports your goals? Yes, please.

1 pound new potatoes, cut into 1-inch cubes
1 large head cauliflower
¼ cup unsweetened almond milk
1 tablespoon unsalted butter
½ teaspoon salt
¼ teaspoon freshly ground black pepper
2 tablespoons chopped fresh chives

1. Put the potatoes in a large pot. Cover with water and bring to a boil over medium-high heat. Cook until the potatoes are tender when pierced with a fork, about 10 minutes. Drain and return the potatoes to the pot.
2. Meanwhile, fill another large pot with a couple inches of water and a steamer basket. Bring the water to a boil over high heat. Add the cauliflower, cover, and steam until tender, 6 to 8 minutes. Drain and add the cauliflower to the pot with the potatoes.
3. Using a potato masher, mash the potatoes and cauliflower together to the desired consistency.
4. Add the almond milk, butter, salt, pepper, and chives and mix well. Serve hot.

Per Serving: Calories: 112; Protein: 4g; Total carbs: 20g; Fiber: 4g; Fat: 2g

CHAPTER 10

Sweets

Banana Cream Pie Parfaits

SERVINGS: 2 / PREP TIME: 15 MINUTES

This lighter take on a classic dessert brings together creamy low-fat vanilla pudding, crunchy graham cracker crumbs, and nutrient-packed bananas and walnuts. It's a satisfying treat that delivers potassium, omega-3s, and a touch of sweetness without going overboard. Perfect for prepping ahead, these parfaits make a crowd-pleasing, guilt-aware dessert for any occasion.

- 1 cup nonfat vanilla pudding
- ½ cup plain or vanilla nonfat Greek yogurt
- 2 graham crackers, crushed
- 1 banana, peeled and sliced
- 2 tablespoons walnuts, chopped, plus more for topping
- Honey for drizzling

1. Mix the vanilla pudding and Greek yogurt together in a bowl.
2. In small parfait dishes or glasses, layer the ingredients, starting with the pudding mix, then crumbs, bananas, and ending with chopped walnuts.
3. You can repeat the layers, depending on the size of the glass and your preferences.
4. Top with a few walnuts and drizzle with the honey. Serve chilled.

Substitution tip: If you don't have graham crackers you can swap in vanilla wafers.

Per Serving: Calories: 255; Protein: 9g; Total carbs: 40g; Fiber: 2g; Fat: 7g

Grilled Peach and Coconut Yogurt Bowls

SERVINGS: 4 / PREP TIME: 5 MINUTES / COOK TIME: 10 MINUTES

Nature's original dessert shines in this simple yet satisfying dish. Grilling peaches caramelizes their natural sweetness, creating a rich flavor without added sugar. Paired with creamy coconut yogurt and crunchy pistachios, it's a refreshing, nutrient-packed treat that satisfies your sweet tooth while supporting your health goals.

2 peaches, halved and pitted
1 cup plain nonfat Greek yogurt
1 teaspoon pure vanilla extract
¼ cup unsweetened dried coconut flakes
2 tablespoons unsalted pistachios, shelled and broken into pieces

1. Preheat the broiler to high. Arrange the rack in the position closest to the broiler.
2. In a shallow pan, arrange the peach halves cut-side up. Broil for 6 to 8 minutes, until browned, tender, and hot.
3. In a small bowl, mix the yogurt and vanilla.
4. Spoon the yogurt into the cavity of each peach half.
5. Sprinkle 1 tablespoon of coconut flakes and 1½ teaspoons of pistachios over each peach half. Serve warm.

Substitution tip: Use other stone fruit in place of peaches, as available. Nectarines, plums, and fresh apricots make great alternatives.

Per Serving: Calories: 122; Protein: 7g; Total carbs: 11g; Fiber: 2g; Fat: 6g

Berry Smoothie Pops

SERVINGS: 6 / PREP TIME: 5 MINUTES, PLUS 3 TO 4 HOURS FOR FREEZING

Berries are a top choice for a sweet treat. They're packed with fiber and antioxidants. Blended with protein-rich Greek yogurt and nutrient-dense hemp seeds, these smoothie pops make for a refreshing, satisfying dessert that's as good for your goals as it is delicious.

2 cups frozen mixed berries
½ cup unsweetened plain almond milk
1 cup plain nonfat Greek yogurt
2 tablespoons hemp seeds

1. Place the berries, milk, yogurt, and hemp seeds in a blender and process until finely blended.
2. Pour the smoothie mixture into 6 clean ice pop molds and insert sticks.
3. Freeze for 3 to 4 hours until firm.

Technique tip: Don't worry if you don't have ice pop molds. You can make these using small cups and ice pop sticks instead. To keep the sticks in place while freezing, arrange the cups on a tray and place the sticks in the smoothies. Cover with a piece of aluminum foil, poking holes in it where the sticks stand to hold them upright until frozen.

Per Serving: Calories: 64; Protein: 5g; Total carbs: 7g; Fiber: 1g; Fat: 2g

Peanut Butter and Banana Power Smoothie

SERVINGS: 2 / PREP TIME: 5 MINUTES

This smoothie packs a protein punch with over 20 grams per serving thanks to whey protein powder and peanut butter. The natural carbs from the banana provide quick energy, balanced by protein. It's a delicious, nutrient-rich way to fuel your day or recover after a workout.

- 1½ cups nonfat plain Greek yogurt
- 1 banana
- 1 teaspoon vanilla extract
- ½ cup ice
- ¼ cup unsweetened dry peanut butter powder
- 1 tablespoon whey protein powder
- ¼ teaspoon maple syrup (optional)

Add the yogurt, banana, vanilla, ice, peanut butter powder, protein powder, and maple syrup (if using) to a blender. Blend on low for about 2 minutes until completely combined. If too thick, thin with water. Enjoy immediately.

Per Serving: Calories: 199; Protein: 25g; Total carbs: 22g; Fiber: 3g; Fat: 1g

Lemon Meringue Pie Smoothie

SERVINGS: 1 / PREP TIME: 5 MINUTES

This creamy, tangy smoothie delivers the sweet and tart flavors of lemon meringue pie while packing a high-protein, low-carb punch to keep your blood sugar steady. It's a perfect treat to satisfy your sweet tooth and support your goals.

¾ cup nonfat plain Greek yogurt
½ cup unsweetened almond milk
Juice of 1 large lemon or 2 small lemons
Grated zest from lemons
1 tablespoon whey protein powder
½ teaspoon vanilla extract
¼ teaspoon maple syrup

Add the yogurt, almond milk, lemon juice, lemon zest, protein powder, vanilla extract, and maple syrup to a blender. Blend on low for about 1 minute until completely combined. Enjoy immediately.

Cooking tip: If you have problems with protein clumping in your smoothie, mix the whey protein powder with almond milk by hand with a fork or whisk first. Then combine this protein shake mixture with yogurt and maple syrup before adding it to the blender.

Per Serving: Calories: 150; Protein: 24g; Total carbs: 11g; Fiber: 0g; Fat: 1g

Creamy Pumpkin Pie Smoothie

SERVINGS: 1 / PREP TIME: 5 MINUTES

Enjoy the cozy flavors of pumpkin spice any time of year with this creamy, protein-packed smoothie. Whey protein and Greek yogurt balance the natural sweetness of the pumpkin and cinnamon spice, making it a satisfying meal option that supports your metabolism and keeps cravings at bay.

- 1 cup nonfat plain Greek yogurt
- ⅔ cup unsweetened canned pumpkin
- 1 tablespoon whey protein powder
- 1¼ teaspoon ground cinnamon
- ½ teaspoon maple syrup (optional)
- Dash salt (optional)

Add the yogurt, pumpkin, protein powder, cinnamon, maple syrup (if using), and salt (if using) to a blender. Blend on low for about 2 minutes until completely combined. Enjoy immediately.

Cooking tip: If you prefer a spicier pumpkin pie flavor, add more cinnamon, a bit of nutmeg, or swap in a pumpkin pie spice blend.

Per Serving: Calories: 257; Protein: 33g; Total carbs: 28g; Fiber: 7g; Fat: 1g

Banana Brûlée Yogurt Parfait

SERVINGS: 1 / PREP TIME: 5 MINUTES / COOK TIME: 2 MINUTES

Craving dessert for breakfast? This parfait delivers just that, with protein-rich yogurt bringing tartness and creaminess, balanced by the caramelized sweetness of cooked bananas. It's a satisfying, nutrient-packed meal that works equally well as a morning boost or an evening treat.

Nonstick cooking spray
¼ cup banana slices
1 teaspoon brown sugar
1 cup nonfat plain Greek yogurt
Dash ground cinnamon

1. Spray a small skillet with cooking spray and place the skillet over medium heat.
2. Place the banana slices in the skillet. Sprinkle the brown sugar over the banana slices. Cook for 1 to 2 minutes, stirring frequently, until heated through. Remove from heat.
3. Place the yogurt into a bowl and pour the banana mixture over the yogurt. Sprinkle with cinnamon and enjoy immediately.

Cooking tip: Be sure to have the ingredients measured out prior to cooking the banana slices, as this mixture will cook fast and may burn if you're not careful.

Per Serving: Calories: 183; Protein: 23g; Total carbs: 21g; Fiber: 1g; Fat: 0g

Chia Chocolate Pudding

SERVINGS: 1 / PREP TIME: 5 MINUTES, PLUS OVERNIGHT TO CHILL

This creamy, chocolaty treat is a dessert classic reimagined. It's packed with protein from Greek yogurt and whey powder. The cocoa satisfies your chocolate cravings while keeping the snack nutrient-dense. A delicious way to enjoy dessert any time of day.

½ cup unsweetened almond milk
½ cup nonfat plain Greek yogurt
½ teaspoon vanilla extract
2 tablespoons chia seeds
1 tablespoon whey protein powder
1 teaspoon unsweetened cocoa powder
½ teaspoon maple syrup

In a canning jar, combine the almond milk, yogurt, vanilla, chia seeds, protein powder, cocoa powder, and maple syrup. Seal with a lid and chill in the refrigerator overnight.

Per Serving: Calories: 263; Protein: 24g; Total carbs: 20g; Fiber: 11g; Fat: 11g

Simply Vanilla Frozen Greek Yogurt

SERVINGS: 4 / PREP TIME: 5 MINUTES, PLUS 8 HOURS TO FREEZE

Can't fit in ice cream while eating for your goals? This homemade frozen Greek yogurt delivers all the creamy, classic vanilla flavor you love without the added sugars and fats. Packed with protein and easily paired with fresh fruit, it's a satisfying, healthy dessert that fits perfectly into your balanced lifestyle.

4 cups nonfat plain Greek yogurt
4 tablespoons whey protein powder
2 tablespoons vanilla extract
2 teaspoons maple syrup

1. In a large bowl or loaf pan, combine the Greek yogurt, protein powder, vanilla, and maple syrup.
2. Cover and freeze overnight or for at least 8 hours. About an hour before serving, set the frozen yogurt in the refrigerator to thaw slightly.

Per Serving: Calories: 128; Protein: 24g; Total carbs: 9g; Fiber: 0g; Fat: 1g

Lemon-Coconut Protein Balls

SERVINGS: 6 / PREP TIME: 10 MINUTES, PLUS 30 MINUTES TO SET

These zesty, portable bites are perfect for fueling your workouts, powering through the afternoon slump, or grabbing a quick breakfast on the go. Packed with protein and healthy fats, they keep hunger at bay and energy steady. If you don't have desiccated coconut, finely ground almonds or pistachios work beautifully as a substitute.

½ cup raw cashews
½ cup prepared peanut butter powder (we like PB2)
1 cup rolled oats
½ cup unsweetened desiccated coconut, divided
1 tablespoon coconut oil
Pinch sea salt
½ cup whey protein powder
Grated zest and juice of 1 medium lemon
¼ cup maple syrup

1. Put the cashews, peanut butter powder, oats, ¼ cup of dessicated coconut, the oil, and the salt in a food processor. Process for about 2 minutes, until fine.
2. Add the protein powder and lemon zest. Pulse until well combined.
3. Add the maple syrup, then slowly add the lemon juice in a thin stream, pulsing until the mixture has a firm but sticky texture.
4. Spread the remaining ¼ cup desiccated coconut on a large plate.
5. Scoop the mixture into 12 individual balls, roll them between your hands until smooth, and then roll each in the coconut to coat evenly.
6. Refrigerate until firm, about 30 minutes, before eating.

Per Serving: Calories: 242; Protein: 13g; Total carbs: 27g; Fiber: 4g; Fat: 10g

Peanut Butter Cup Smoothie

SERVINGS: 2 / PREP TIME: 5 MINUTES

If you love the classic combo of chocolate and peanut butter, this smoothie delivers those flavors in a nourishing, protein-packed way. Perfect for breakfast or a satisfying snack, it's a delicious treat that supports your goals while satisfying your sweet tooth.

1 cup water
¾ cup skim milk
1 tablespoon whey protein powder
1 teaspoon cocoa powder
2 tablespoons natural peanut butter
½ teaspoon maple syrup
3 ice cubes

Place the water, milk, protein powder, cocoa powder, peanut butter, maple syrup, and ice in a blender and blend until smooth. Pour into 2 glasses and serve immediately.

Per Serving: Calories: 157; Protein: 10g; Total carbs: 6g; Fiber: 2g; Fat: 10g

Greek Yogurt and Marinated Pineapple

SERVINGS: 4 / PREP TIME: 10 MINUTES, PLUS AT LEAST 4 HOURS TO MARINATE

This simple, refreshing dessert is as nutritious as it is delicious. Greek yogurt provides a solid protein boost, while the pineapple adds natural sweetness and its enzymes support digestion. Marinate the pineapple ahead of time to let the flavors deepen, if you're looking for a perfect make-ahead treat that keeps your goals on track.

- 1 cup fresh pineapple, diced
- ¼ cup no-sugar added pineapple juice
- 1 tablespoon freshly squeezed lemon juice
- 1 teaspoon grated lemon zest
- 1 tablespoon chopped mint
- 1 teaspoon honey
- 1 teaspoon vanilla extract
- 2 cups nonfat plain Greek yogurt
- Fresh mint leaves, for garnish (optional)

1. In a small bowl, combine the pineapple, pineapple juice, lemon juice, lemon zest, mint, honey, and vanilla. Mix well.
2. Spoon the mixture into a quart-size zippered plastic bag and shake a few times after sealing. Allow the pineapple mixture to marinate in the fridge for at least 4 hours, preferably overnight, shaking gently two or three times.
3. Spoon ½ cup of Greek yogurt into each of four dessert dishes and top with ¼ cup of the pineapple topping. Garnish with fresh mint leaves, if desired.

Per Serving: Calories: 109; Protein: 11g; Total carbs: 10g; Fiber: 1g; Fat: 2g

Orange and Whipped-Cheese Dessert Cups

SERVINGS: 4 / PREP TIME: 15 MINUTES / COOK TIME: 5 MINUTES

Simple to make but delightfully decadent, these dessert cups offer the creamy richness of cheesecake with far less sugar. Their bright citrus flavor and elegant presentation make them perfect for entertaining, or a special treat just for you.

1 cup part-skim ricotta cheese
1 cup low-fat cream cheese
2 tablespoons honey, plus 2 teaspoons, divided
2 tablespoons low-fat milk
½ teaspoon vanilla extract
½ teaspoon ground cinnamon
½ teaspoon allspice
¼ teaspoon nutmeg
3 large navel oranges, sectioned, membrane removed
Fresh basil leaves, for garnish

1. In a blender or food processor, combine the ricotta, cream cheese, 2 tablespoons of honey, milk, vanilla, and cinnamon, and process until smooth.
2. Spoon the cheese mixture into four dessert cups, cover, and refrigerate for at least 10 minutes to chill.
3. In a medium skillet, heat the remaining 2 teaspoons of honey on low until thin and warm. Stir in the allspice and nutmeg until well mixed.
4. Add the orange slices and cook for 1 minute. Gently tum the orange slices over and cook for 1 to 2 minutes or until just beginning to brown. Remove from heat.
5. Allow the orange slices to cool to room temperature, then top each dessert dish with ¼ of the oranges. To serve, garnish each cup with a basil leaf.

Per Serving: Calories: 310; Protein: 9g; Total carbs: 34g; Fiber: 2g; Fat: 15g

Fruit Kabobs with Dark Chocolate Drizzle

SERVINGS: 4 / PREP TIME: 30 MINUTES / COOK TIME: 10 MINUTES

These colorful fruit kabobs are a crowd-pleaser for kids and adults alike. They are easy to make, refreshing, and naturally sweet. The dark chocolate drizzle adds just the right touch of indulgence without going overboard. Serve them fondue-style at parties for a fun, interactive dessert. For this recipe you'll need eight bamboo skewers, soaked in water for 30 minutes.

1 cantaloupe, peeled and cut into chunks
1 honeydew melon, peeled and cut into chunks
1 pound fresh strawberries, capped
½ cup 2% milk
1 cup dark chocolate chips
1 teaspoon vanilla extract

1. Preheat the broiler to high and line a baking sheet with aluminum foil.
2. Thread the cantaloupe, melon, and strawberries onto the skewers in an alternating pattern and place the skewers on the baking sheet. Broil for 2 minutes, turn, and broil for an additional 2 minutes.
3. Meanwhile, heat the milk in a small saucepan on medium-low heat until steaming, but not foamy and boiled, about 5 minutes.
4. Place the chocolate chips in a large glass bowl and pour the milk over the chips. Add the vanilla and stir until melted and smooth.
5. Remove the fruit kabobs from the oven and place them on a platter. Drizzle with the chocolate sauce and serve.

Per Serving: Calories: 190; Protein: 4g; Total carbs: 30g; Fiber: 2g; Fat: 5g

Red-Wine Poached Pears

SERVINGS: 2 / PREP TIME: 5 MINUTES / COOK TIME: 25 MINUTES

These tender, fiber-rich pears are poached to perfection in red wine for a dessert that feels indulgent but stays light. Pair them with nonfat Greek yogurt for a balanced, nutrient-packed treat, or serve alongside savory dishes to add a touch of natural sweetness and sophistication to your meal.

2 cups red wine, such as merlot or zinfandel, plus more if necessary
2 firm pears, peeled
2 or 3 cardamom pods, split
1 cinnamon stick
2 peppercorns
1 bay leaf

1. In a large pot, combine the wine, pears, cardamom, cinnamon, peppercorns, and bay leaf, making sure the pears are submerged in the wine. Bring to a boil.
2. Reduce the heat and simmer for 15 to 20 minutes, until the pears are tender when poked with a fork. Remove the pears from the wine and allow them to cool.
3. Bring the wine to a boil and cook until it reduces to a syrup, about 10 minutes. Strain into a glass bowl.
4. Drizzle the pears with the warmed syrup before serving.

Per Serving: Calories: 115; Protein: 1g; Total carbs: 14g; Fiber: 6g; Fat: 0g

MEASUREMENT CONVERSIONS

VOLUME EQUIVALENTS	U.S. STANDARD	U.S. STANDARD (OUNCES)	METRIC (APPROXIMATE)
LIQUID	2 tablespoons	1 fl. oz.	30 mL
	¼ cup	2 fl. oz.	60 mL
	½ cup	4 fl. oz.	120 mL
	1 cup	8 fl. oz.	240 mL
	1½ cups	12 fl. oz.	355 mL
	2 cups or 1 pint	16 fl. oz.	475 mL
	4 cups or 1 quart	32 fl. oz.	1 L
	1 gallon	128 fl. oz.	4 L
DRY	⅛ teaspoon	—	0.5 mL
	¼ teaspoon	—	1 mL
	½ teaspoon	—	2 mL
	¾ teaspoon	—	4 mL
	1 teaspoon	—	5 mL
	1 tablespoon	—	15 mL
	¼ cup	—	59 mL
	⅓ cup	—	79 mL
	½ cup	—	118 mL
	⅔ cup	—	156 mL
	¾ cup	—	177 mL
	1 cup	—	235 mL
	2 cups or 1 pint	—	475 mL
	3 cups	—	700 mL
	4 cups or 1 quart	—	1 L
	½ gallon	—	2 L
	1 gallon	—	4 L

OVEN TEMPERATURES

FAHRENHEIT	CELSIUS (APPROXIMATE)
250°F	120°C
300°F	150°C
325°F	165°C
350°F	180°C
375°F	190°C
400°F	200°C
425°F	220°C
450°F	230°C

WEIGHT EQUIVALENTS

U.S. STANDARD	METRIC (APPROXIMATE)
½ ounce	15 g
1 ounce	30 g
2 ounces	60 g
4 ounces	115 g
8 ounces	225 g
12 ounces	340 g
16 ounces or 1 pound	455 g

RESOURCES

Here are some trusted resources to help you dig deeper into GLP-1 medications, protein-forward nutrition, metabolism, and sustainable weight management.

Books

Burn by Herman Pontzer, PhD. Explores how the human body uses energy, challenging old weight-loss myths.

The Obesity Code by Jason Fung, MD. Offers insight into insulin resistance and metabolic health.

Roar by Stacy T. Sims, PhD, with Selene Yeager. Especially helpful for women, this book explains how to fuel workouts and adapt nutrition across life stages.

Podcasts

FoundMyFitness with Dr. Rhonda Patrick. Deep dives into metabolism, protein, exercise, and aging.

The *Huberman Lab* podcast. Offers science-based strategies for behavior change, sleep, exercise, and neurobiology.

Apps

MyFitnessPal or MacrosFirst. For those who want to track protein or overall macros with flexibility. The free version of MacrosFirst has great features without paying for premium.

WaterMinder. A helpful hydration reminder that makes daily water intake easier to manage.

Find More of Us Online

glp1enhanced.com. Our main site for access to our full programs (GLP1 Enhanced Nutrition Blueprint for those getting ready to start medication or already on it who are looking to maximize fat loss and maintain muscle, and Master Your Taper for those who are almost at their goal, planning to taper their dose, and wanting to maintain their results without gaining all the weight back), our recipe bundle, and our strength training plan.

Instagram: @glp1enhanced. Follow us for great tips, workout inspiration, and real-life support from people who get it.

TikTok: @glp1enhanced

Facebook: GLP1 Enhanced

These resources can help you stay informed and empowered as you continue building the habits and mindset that lead to long-term success.

REFERENCES

Davies, Melanie, Louise Færch, Ole K. Jeppesen, Arash Pakseresht, Sue D. Pedersen, Leigh Perreault, Julio Rosenstock, et al. "Semaglutide 2.4 mg once a week in adults with overweight or obesity, and type 2 diabetes (Step 2): A randomised, double-blind, double-dummy, placebo-controlled, Phase 3 trial." *The Lancet* 397, no. 10278 (2021): 971–84. https://doi.org/10.1016/S0140-6736(21)00213-0.

Drucker, Daniel J. "Mechanisms of action and therapeutic application of glucagon-like peptide-1." *Cell Metabolism* 27, no. 4 (2018):740–56. doi: 10.1016/j.cmet.2018.03.001. PMID: 29617641.

Hall, Kevin D., Gary Sacks, Dhruva Chandramohan, Carson C. Chow, Y. Claire Wang, Steven L. Gortmaker, Boyd A. Swinburn. "Quantification of the effect of energy imbalance on bodyweight." *The Lancet* 378, no. 9793 (2011):826–37. doi: 10.1016/S0140-6736(11)60812-X. PMID: 21872751; PMCID: PMC3880593.

Harris, Kira B. and Delilah J. McCarty. "Efficacy and tolerability of glucagon-like peptide-1 receptor agonists in patients with type 2 diabetes mellitus." *Therapeutic Advances in Endocrinology and Metabolism* 6, no. 1 (2015):3–18. doi: 10.1177/2042018814558242. PMID: 25678952; PMCID: PMC4321868.

Layman , Donald K., Ellen Evans, Jamie I. Baum, Jennifer Seyler, Donna J. Erickson, and Richard A. Boileau. "Dietary protein and exercise have additive effects on body composition during weight loss in adult women." *The Journal of Nutrition 135,* no. 8 (2005):1903–10. doi: 10.1093/jn/135.8.1903. PMID: 16046715.

Lowe, Michael R. and Meghan L. Butryn. "Hedonic hunger: A new dimension of appetite?" *Physiology & Behavior*. 2007 Jul 24;91(4):432–9. doi: 10.1016/j.physbeh.2007.04.006. Epub (2007). PMID: 17531274.

Marx, Nikolaus, Mansoor Husain, Michael Lehrke, Subodh Verma, and Naveed Sattar. "GLP-1 receptor agonists for the reduction of atherosclerotic cardiovascular risk in patients with type 2 diabetes." *Circulation* 146, no. 24 (2022): 1882–94. https://doi.org/doi:10.1161/CIRCULATIONAHA.122.059595.

Nauck, Michael A. and Juris J. Meier. "Incretin hormones: Their role in health and disease." *Diabetes, Obesity and Metabolism* 20, no. 1 (2018):5-21. doi: 10.1111/dom.13129. PMID: 29364588.

Nauck, Michael A. and Juris J. Meier. "The incretin effect in healthy individuals and those with type 2 diabetes: Physiology, pathophysiology, and response to therapeutic interventions." *The Lancet Diabetes & Endocrinology* 4, no. 6 (2016):525–36. doi: 10.1016/S2213-8587(15)00482-9. Epub 2016 Feb 12. PMID: 26876794.

Nauck, Michael A., Daniel R. Quast, Jakob Wefers, Juris J. Meier. "GLP-1 receptor agonists in the treatment of type 2 diabetes - state-of-the-art." *Molecular Metabolism*. 2021 Apr; 46:101102. doi: 10.1016/j.molmet.2020.101102. Epub (2020). PMID: 33068776; PMCID: PMC8085572.

Phillips, Stuart M., Stéphanie Chevalier, Heather J. Leidy. "Protein 'requirements' beyond the RDA: Implications for optimizing health." *Applied Physiology, Nutrition, and Metabolism* 41, no. 5 (2016):565–72. doi: 10.1139/apnm-2015-0550. Epub (2016). Erratum in: *Applied Physiology, Nutrition, and Metabolism* 47, no. 5 (2022):615. doi: 10.1139/apnm-2022-0131. PMID: 26960445.

Piercy , Katrina L., Richard P. Troiano, Rachel M. Ballard, Susan A. Carlson, Janet E. Fulton, Deborah A. Galuska, Stephanie M. George, Richard D. Olson. "The physical activity guidelines for Americans." *JAMA* 320, no. 19 (2018):2020–8 doi: 10.1001/jama.2018.14854. PMID: 30418471; PMCID: PMC9582631.

Stokes , Tanner, Amy J. Hector, Robert W. Morton, Chris McGlory, Stuart M. Phillips. "Recent perspectives regarding the role of dietary protein for the promotion of muscle hypertrophy with resistance exercise training." *Nutrients* 10, no. 2 (2018):180. doi: 10.3390/nu10020180. PMID: 29414855; PMCID: PMC5852756.

Warburton, Darren E. R., Crystal W. Nicol, Shannon S. D. Bredin. "Health benefits of physical activity: The evidence. " *Canadian Medical Association Journal* 174, no. 6 (2006):801-9. doi: 10.1503/cmaj.051351. PMID: 16534088; PMCID: PMC1402378.

Wilding , John P. H., D.M., Rachel L. Batterham, Salvatore Calanna, Melanie Davies, Luc F. Van Gaal, Ildiko Lingvay, Barbara M. McGowan, Julio Rosenstock, Marie T. D. Tran, Thomas A. Wadden, Sean Wharton, Koutaro Yokote, Niels Zeuthen, Robert F. Kushner for the STEP 1 Study Group. "Once-weekly semaglutide in adults with overweight or obesity." *The New England Journal of Medicine* 384, no. 11 (2021):989–1002. doi: 10.1056/NEJMoa2032183. Epub 2021 Feb 10. PMID: 33567185.

Wolfe, Robert R. "The underappreciated role of muscle in health and disease." *The American Journal of Clinical Nutrition* 84, no. 3 (2006):475–82. doi: 10.1093/ajcn/84.3.475. PMID: 16960159.

INDEX

C

D

E

F

G

P

Q

R

S

T

Acknowledgments

This book is the result of many hours, conversations, and cups of coffee, and we're so grateful to the people who helped bring it to life. To our families: Thank you for your love, patience, and support (and for tolerating a lot of protein talk). To our clients and community: You're the reason we do this work. Your determination, honesty, and growth inspire us every single day. To our team at Callisto Publishing: Thank you for believing in this message and helping us shape it into something useful, encouraging, and real. And to each other: Thank you for the laughter, late nights, and shared vision. We're so proud of what we've built, and even more excited for what's ahead.

—Aliza & Kellie

About the Authors

Aliza Olive, MD, is a pediatric intensivist, nutrition coach, and co-founder of GLP1 Enhanced. She specializes in helping people lose fat and maintain muscle while on or tapering off GLP-1 medications.

Kellie Bader, PharmD, is a clinical pharmacist, certified nutrition coach, and co-founder of GLP1 Enhanced. She's passionate about making high-protein eating simple, satisfying, and sustainable.

Together, Aliza and Kellie bring years of combined experience in medicine, pharmacology, nutrition, and coaching to their clients and community. Through their signature programs, they help people break plateaus, reverse metabolic adaptation, and maintain their results long after the medication ends.